T0316652

Cambridge Elements ≡

Elements in the Philosophy of Religion
edited by
Yujin Nagasawa
University of Birmingham

THE DIVINE ATTRIBUTES

T. J. Mawson
Oxford University

CAMBRIDGE
UNIVERSITY PRESS

University Printing House, Cambridge CB2 8BS, United Kingdom

One Liberty Plaza, 20th Floor, New York, NY 10006, USA

477 Williamstown Road, Port Melbourne, VIC 3207, Australia

314–321, 3rd Floor, Plot 3, Splendor Forum, Jasola District Centre, New Delhi – 110025, India

79 Anson Road, #06–04/06, Singapore 079906

Cambridge University Press is part of the University of Cambridge.

It furthers the University's mission by disseminating knowledge in the pursuit of education, learning, and research at the highest international levels of excellence.

www.cambridge.org
Information on this title: www.cambridge.org/9781108468336
DOI: 10.1017/9781108598101

First published 2019

A catalogue record for this publication is available from the British Library.

ISBN 978-1-108-46833-6 Paperback
ISSN 2399-5165 (online)
ISSN 2515-9763 (print)

The Divine Attributes

DOI: 10.1017/9781108598101
First published online: December 2018

T. J. Mawson
Oxford University

Abstract: *The Divine Attributes* explores the traditional theistic concept of God as the most perfect being possible, discussing the main divine attributes which flow from this understanding – personhood, transcendence, immanence, omnipresence, omniscience, omnipotence, perfect goodness, unity, simplicity and necessity. It argues that the atemporalist's conception of God is to be preferred over the temporalist's on the grounds of Perfect Being Theology, but that, if it were to be the case that the temporal God existed, rather than the atemporal God, He'd still be 'perfect enough' to count as the God of theism.

Keywords: God, theism, divine attributes, atemporalism, temporalism

ISBNs: 9781108468336 (PB) 9781108598101 (OC)
ISSNs: 2399–5165 (online) 2515–9763 (print)

Contents

Preface

I would like to start by thanking all who have helped me with this Element. But I can only draw out for explicit mention some of them. John Cottingham, Stewart Goetz, Brian Leftow, Martin Pickup, Richard Swinburne and Bill Wood have been kind enough to read the first draft in its entirety or read sections of it and offer comments which have enabled me to improve on it. The anonymous reviewer for CUP was also tremendously helpful; he or she really did go above and beyond the call of duty.

Second, I should offer the reader some apologies in advance.

There are many properties[1] of God that I do not as much as mention in this Element. I have had to narrow my focus to considering only essential attributes of God and of course I have not been able to consider even all of those. I do not even try to discuss God's accidental attributes. Insofar as they come up, they do so as I attempt to use them to illuminate the essential attributes of God. There are accidental attributes of God which, despite that status, almost all theists agree that God has. The most significant of these are creator of the natural world; source of value for us; revealer of Himself and His will; and offerer of eternal life. Some of these accidental attributes may be thought to be more important to the relevance of God to our lives than at least some of the essential attributes that I do discuss. And thus they may be thought more worthy of discussion than at least some of these attributes. In addition, what I say about the essential attributes that I consider is, in some cases, so brief as to be embarrassing to me. I have had to strip out many notes citing works which, were they to be consulted by my readers, would go to make up some of that shortfall. And I have had to strip out everything from the Bibliography other than details of the works which I have actually cited.[2] The explanation for such omissions is of course the need to make hard choices in the light of the word limit imposed by the publisher, but I offer my apologies nonetheless. Additionally, I apologise for the lack of an index; this has been omitted to conform with the required style for Elements.

And then there is the incompleteness of the case that I make in favour of atemporalism and against temporalism as ways of conceptualising the theistic God. As I develop this case in this Element, I point to various ways in which it is less than conclusive and, in that I think the correct analysis of the best arguments available in this area is that any such case really is inconclusive, I'm not apologising for that. But there is one significant way in which the

---

[1] In this volume, I use the words 'property' and 'attribute' synonymously.

[2] In this context then, may I draw interested readers' attention to two works, which, as I do cite them, do manage to appear in the Bibliography as it is – that of Hoffman and Rosenkrantz and that of Oppy. Each is more comprehensive than this slender book could ever hope to be.

analysis of the situation given in this Element is incomplete. According to my analysis, the temporal God, while falling short of the atemporal when it comes to what it's logically possible the greatest person might be, does not fall so far short that we should say he's only a god, not God.[3] If in fact, of metaphysical necessity, the best person possible is the temporal God and such a being exists, it's still God that exists. It's just that God is less great than it's logically possible He could have been. He's still as great as it's metaphysically possible anyone might be.[4] And if that's right, it means that the temporalist may fairly push back at the atemporalist on grounds which fall outside the purview of this Element and thus which I do not survey as the Element progresses. But allow me to look over the border at these grounds before I move on to make what progress I am able on the ground, and in the time, allotted to me.

Apart from issues to do with the consistency of the concept of God, the main reason people cite against the existence of God is the problem of evil. It's not at all implausible to think that the temporalist can turn what seems to me to be a weakness when thinking about the concept of God (the temporal God is less great than the atemporal) into a strength when arguing for His existence in the face of evil (God is less great than atemporalists have supposed Him to be). I shall suggest that a temporal God would know little, if anything, about the future; would not be truly all-powerful, as a result; would be well intentioned, but prone to bodging; and would thus be dependent on the vagaries of luck for how beneficent and virtuous (if not benevolent) He managed to end up being. Such a God is one that it is plausible to think it will be harder to gain evidence against the existence of from a world such as ours. Indeed, one might say that *this* – indicating the world by pointing at some of the worst bits of it – is just the sort of world that such a God would stick us with! If that's right, then if a perfect being's essential attributes could not – of metaphysical necessity – be as good as I shall argue they could be as a matter of logical possibility, the rationality of believing in God may be rather greater than many suppose it to be.

---

[3] In this work, I use the capital 'G' to indicate that the being in question is the God of theism, whom I understand to be the most perfect being possible and I use a small 'g' to indicate otherwise. So, were there a being like Zeus, he would be a god (possibly even the only god), but not God. Similarly, I use 'He' – capitalised – rather than 'he' (or 'She' etc.) to refer to the God of theism. These are all issues of taxonomic and stylistic preference; nothing of substance turns on them.

[4] In this Element, I use an understanding of metaphysical necessity as something stronger than physical necessity, but less strong than logical necessity; in terms of possible worlds, there are logically possible worlds which are not metaphysically possible, but no metaphysically possible worlds which are not logically possible. In such a case as is envisaged in the Element, the atemporal God would exist in some logically possible worlds, but not in any metaphysically possible ones; the temporal God would exist in all metaphysically possible worlds. This understanding is defended in section 3.

Introduction: Perfect Being Theology

Throughout history (and, no doubt, pre-history) different people have attributed different properties to God. And this diversity of opinion persists in popular culture even to the present day. However, within the discipline of philosophy, things are better regulated, as one would have hoped.

Two-and-a-half thousand years of philosophical speculation as to the nature of the God worshipped by the main monotheistic religions – Judaism, Christianity and Islam – has honed a concept of God. The resultant concept – the theistic concept, as it has become known – is now more or less uniformly the concept of God that is in the minds of those who are philosophically informed when they declare either that that they believe in God (are theists) or that they do not (are atheists or agnostics). In order to make progress in the relatively short space that is available to me in this Element, I shall thus narrow my focus to the most central of the essential divine attributes as they are understood in the theistic tradition. Even then I shall have to be somewhat stipulative in how I take that tradition.

Typical of the theistic tradition are the two most significant philosophers of religion of the twentieth century (and, so far, the twenty-first), Alvin Plantinga and Richard Swinburne. They write thus:

> God is a *person*; that is, a being with intellect and will. A person has (or can have) knowledge and belief, but also affections, loves, and hates; a person, furthermore, also has or can have intentions, and can act so as to fulfil them. God has all these qualities and has some (knowledge, power, and love, for example) to the maximal degree. God is thus all-knowing and all-powerful; He is also perfectly good and wholly loving. Still further, he has created the universe and constantly upholds and providentially guides it. This is the *theistic* component of Christian belief.[5]
>
> By 'theism' I understand the doctrine that there is a God in the sense of a being with most of the following properties: being a person without a body (that is, a spirit), present everywhere (that is, omnipresent), the creator of the universe, perfectly free, able to do anything (that is, omnipotent), knowing all things (that is, omniscient), perfectly good, a source of moral obligation, eternal, a necessary being, holy, and worthy of worship.[6]

Within the theistic tradition, there is variation in how the concept of God is understood, the most significant division, I shall argue, being between those who see God's eternality as His being outside time and those who see it as His being inside time but everlasting in both the backwards and forwards direction, which difference of opinion has knock-on effects for how other divine attributes are to be understood. If I am not to leave the reader languishing at the

---

[5] A. Plantinga, *Warranted Christian Belief* (Oxford: Oxford University Press, 2000), vii.
[6] R. Swinburne, *The Coherence of Theism*, 2nd edn (Oxford: Oxford University Press, 2016), 1.

level of telling him or her merely how it is that various philosophers have understood the divine attributes, but rather to raise him or her to the level of telling him or her about what are the divine attributes (if God exists), I shall need some sort of 'regulative idea', as it were, to guide me (and him or her). That is to say, I shall need a principle by which to evaluate differing streams of thought within this tradition as more or less commendable, as more or less likely to be true reflections of the attributes God has, or would have were He to exist. In this Element, I'm going to take Perfect Being Theology as that regulative idea. What is Perfect Being Theology? Or, more precisely, how am I going to be taking it?

According to Perfect Being Theology, we should be guided in our thinking about the divine attributes by the thought that God, were He to exist, would have to be the most perfect being possible. God, were He to exist, would have to be a being greater than which none other could be and, given that the sorts of reasons that might prevent a greater being existing could not properly be a part of the natural order, we may perhaps even say that God would have to be a being greater than which none other could even be *conceived*. That is certainly how Anselm famously characterised God – '*aliquid quo nihil maius cogitari possit*' – though he was by no means the first to do so (Seneca and St Augustine used similar formulas). Indeed, Perfect Being Theology has a lineage which goes back to the founding of our discipline. We find examples of it in Plato. In *The Republic*, for example, Plato rates certain stories about God behaving badly as 'objectionable', objectionable not only because of the likely deleterious consequences on young men hearing them (though those consequences are uppermost in Plato's mind), but also because such stories do not adequately reflect the likely nature of God, should He exist. In response to being asked what sort of Theology should then be practised, Plato answers that 'God is always to be represented as he truly is ... And is he not truly good?'. He then goes on to deploy some perfect-being argumentation to reach the conclusion that God must thus be said to be 'not the author of evil, but of good only'.[7] Similar arguments occurring down the generations and up to the present day have cumulatively resulted in the theistic concept of God as sketched by Plantinga and Swinburne in the quotations from their works which I gave a moment ago.[8]

---

[7] Plato, *Republic* Book II, lines 379ff. I use the Jowett translation (B. Jowett, *The Dialogues of Plato* (Oxford: Oxford University Press, 1875), vol. II, 251–3) Of course, in my exegesis, I have assumed which of the views expressed in it are Plato's own and on this (as on much else) there may be dispute.

[8] Oppy says at one stage that 'if one is able to acknowledge that there can be reasonable and informed disagreement about whether God is the greatest possible being, then one can hardly think that it is a conceptual truth – part of the very concept of God – that God is the greatest possible being' (G. Oppy, *Describing Gods* (Cambridge: Cambridge University Press, 2014),

Perfect Being Theology sets up then what we might follow Michael Murray and Michael Rea in calling a 'recipe for developing a more specific conception of God'.[9] The recipe has stages and goes like this. Consider any given attribute, A: think about whether or not having A makes a given thing better or worse than not having it. If better, then 'in it goes'. God should be conceived as having A, at least at the first stage of perfect-being reasoning – of later stages, more later. If it is 'degreed' – that is if it is the sort of attribute that admits of degrees – and if these degrees are such that the more, the better, then He should be conceived of as having A to the greatest extent possible, 'maximally', as it is sometimes put, again at least at the first stage of perfect-being reasoning. 'In it goes', to the maximum extent possible. If having A makes a thing worse, then the opposite. God should be conceived of as lacking A, at the first stage. So, that ingredient stays out. If neither better, nor worse, then we must suspend judgement (or decide on other grounds) on whether or not to include it. And thus we may continue following the recipe for developing our idea of God. Consider power. Is it better to have power or lack it? Obviously, it is better to have power and obviously the more power, the better. So, prima facie, God should be considered the most powerful being possible; He should be thought of as omnipotent. Is it better to know something or be ignorant of it? Obviously, it is better to know something and obviously the more one knows, the better. So, prima facie,

---

16–17). On my account, if someone says that he or she wonders whether or not God (rather than perhaps merely a god) might fail to be the greatest possible being in any sense of 'possible' at all, he or she really is revealing, not perhaps that he or she is unreasonable or ill-informed, but that he or she is using the term 'God' in a way that differs from the usage which would place him or her interior to the theistic tradition in which this work locates itself. But of course I admit – as I started the <u>Introduction</u> by suggesting – *this is stipulative*; outside the confines of this tradition (as so stipulated), the word 'God' is used in different ways. And even interior to the tradition, two different senses of possibility are in play – logical and metaphysical – which complicates matters. If the greatest being that's logically possible is also metaphysically possible, then not much turns on this ambiguity; and the position that the greatest being that's logically possible is also metaphysically possible is in fact the one that most in the tradition have 'occupied' (even if the quotation marks may be justified as arguably they've occupied it by default, not having distinguished between logical and metaphysical possibility). But it's arguably epistemically possible that the greatest being that's logically possible is not metaphysically possible, and thus – interior to the tradition as demarcated – there is room for saying that God is not the greatest possible (meaning logically possible) being even though He is the greatest possible (meaning metaphysically possible) being. That's in fact what I would say is the case if the temporal God exists, rather than the atemporal. Another complication is that it's arguably epistemically possible that the greatest being that's logically or metaphysically possible is not perfect, meaning – the way I divide things up – that one might in consistency say that the greatest being (logically or metaphysically) possible is not God. That is because, as I conceive of the tradition, theism commits itself to *Perfect* Being Theology (not just Greatest Being Theology), though there is some of what I shall call 'well, I suppose I meant "as perfect as possible" wriggle room' here; but I would agree that this too is at least somewhat stipulative.

9 M. Murray and M. Rea, *Introduction to the Philosophy of Religion* (Cambridge: Cambridge University Press, 2008), 8.

God should be considered maximally knowledgeable; He should be thought of as omniscient. And goodness? Well, good intentions are obviously better than bad; good outcomes are better than bad; and good character traits better than bad. And that which is relatively good is better than that which is relatively bad even if the latter is in itself good. So, prima facie, we should think of God as perfectly good – omnibenevolent, omnibeneficent and supremely virtuous. And so on.

The reason for the 'prima facie's' in some of these claims and for the mention of a 'first stage' of perfect-being reasoning is that there may be some attributes that are great-making but that it's not even logically possible to have alongside other great-making attributes. And, if that 'may be' is in fact our starting epistemic position on what we ultimately come to see is of conceptual necessity a 'must be', then, in order to see Perfect Being Theology through to the end, we'll have to do our best to consider sets of logically co-possible attributes and judge which set it is the having of which would make the being in question the best possible, the results of that consideration meaning that *ultima facie* a certain great-making attribute is not one we can attribute to God. Leftow calls this comparison between sets the 'last stage of perfect-being reasoning' and he puts the point in the following way:

> Given that there is the live possibility of conflict for any *prima facie* 'great-making' property, it is a live option that the last stage of perfect-being reasoning (taking us from *prima* to *ultima facie* ascription of a property) rule against it. So . . . something could lack a particular . . . great-making property . . . *because* [emphasis supplied] it is the greatest possible being. For the greatest possible being has the greatest compossible set of great-making attributes, and perhaps that particular great-making property is not compossible with one it is even greater to have.[10]

As well as the sort of case Leftow has in mind, there are a couple of other possibilities, ones which it is as well to flag up at this stage.

First, there is the possibility (at least an epistemic possibility) that two sets of great-making attributes might be different from one another in their members but not evaluable such that one comes out as better than the other, either because both come out as equally good or because they are incommensurable with one another in such a way that they cannot be ranked (other than relative to other sets (as above them)). Let me give a 'toy' example to illustrate.

For simplicity of model, allow me to suppose that there are only two great-making attributes, *A* and *B*; that they logically exclude one another; and

---

[10] B. Leftow, 'Why Perfect Being Theology?', *International Journal for Philosophy of Religion* (2001), 69(2), 103–18, 117.

that each is as exactly as great-making as the other. Allow me also to suppose, again just to keep things simple, that they're not degreed attributes. On these suppositions, the A-attribute-having God and the B-attribute-having God would – *ex hypothesi* – be equally great and it not be possible for anything to be greater, so Perfect Being Theology alone could not tell us whether God had attribute A or B (even assuming it were granted that God exists, which result itself is not something Perfect Being Theology could deliver).[11] We could of course say that, in such a circumstance, God would have the disjunctive attribute of 'having either A or B', but to proceed further to specify quite how He manifested that disjunctive attribute – the A-way or the B-way – we would need to turn to special revelation or to some natural phenomenon as providing evidence. Leibniz, who was one of the first to vex himself (and others) over these sorts of things, would disagree. Leibniz would maintain, via his Principle of Sufficient Reason, that, if there were a God, then there'd have to be some explanation for His having of whichever of A or B it is that He did have. It couldn't just ultimately be an inexplicable contingency. But, as the way that my model has been set up, it *would* have to be an ultimately inexplicable contingency whichever of them He had, then there could not be such a case as I am seeking to model. There is indeed a tradition that precedes Leibniz and runs broader and arguably deeper than the stream of philosophical reflection which he represents, one which anathematises thinking of *any* of God's attributes as contingent. But Leibniz and this broader tradition err.

Contingency should be admitted into God's (non-essential) attributes; He's no less perfect for that. A quick way to see this may be the following.[12] God is perfectly free (in the libertarian sense) and specifically He could have done otherwise than He did in creating this universe – He might have remained the sole existent or created another universe instead of this one. That being so, theists are committed to thinking that the attribute that God has of being creator of this universe is one that He holds contingently. Similarly, if the model that I've been using were to reflect reality in its salient points and there were to be a God, then one might even say that the full specification of the set of attributes the having of which made God the greatest (i.e. one that specified how the disjunctive attribute A-*or*-B was instantiated) would be contingent.[13]

---

[11] *Pace* Anselm.   [12] If one doesn't accept the assumptions, it won't be.

[13] Would this be to admit contingency into the essence of God? No, if one is permitted to say that the relevant essential attribute of God in such a case would be A-*or*-B and that the particular 'specification', as I am putting it, of that property – that He's an A-God, say, rather than a B-God – is what is contingent and non-essential. It's non-essential, as the most perfect being possible would still have been that even had He had this essential property made specific in the B-way. This is a bit like something's having as an essential property *being coloured*, but there being no particular colour that the thing has to have.

If I am right that a perfect being would have some attributes contingently, that entails that Perfect Being Theology faces another limitation and this one, unlike the first situation discussed, is not plausibly merely an epistemic possibility; it's an actuality. The first situation required us to hypothesise that there might be two or more distinct sets of great-making features such that they tie for top place – the having of one set is no better than the having of any of the others. This could be argued to be a mere epistemic possibility; great-making features can't really work this way; the 'possibility' that they might work this way is just an epistemic one – an artefact of our not seeing them clearly enough. As I have said, Leibniz would have diagnosed the situation this way, but others would too. And nothing I have said should be taken to indicate that I am not sympathetic to that thought. I'm just not sympathetic to it as a result of thinking that, were such to obtain, it would require positing contingency in a perfect being and contingency in a perfect being is to be eschewed. Be that as it may, the second sort of situation, to which I'm about to turn, is one which, I shall argue, is not plausibly merely an epistemic possibility; it's something we can know to be actual.

There are some attributes the having of which isn't evaluable at all for a perfect being, so such attributes are not evaluable as great-making (or as bad-making). Perfect Being Theology can't tell us whether or not God has such attributes. An example might be the attribute of having a favourite colour (rather than being indifferent between colours). Some people have a favourite colour; some don't. Those who do aren't *eo ipso* either better or worse than those who do not. And then, among those who do have a favourite colour, there is no colour the having of which as one's favourite makes one better than one would have been had one had any other colour as one's favourite. If we add to this the claim that there are an infinity of colours (there are, after all, an infinity of shades of any one colour), then there are an infinite number of sets of attributes that a perfect being might have and Perfect Being Theology alone won't allow us to adjudicate between them.

Some perfect-being reasoners argue that if a being having a given property would neither add to nor detract from its greatness, we should conclude that God does not have that property, not that Perfect Being Theology can't tell us whether or not He has it. Mander, for example, says, 'A perfect being could have no particular interests or likes. He could not, for instance, have a favourite colour.'[14] But this just seems wrong to me. All that follows from a being's being perfect and its being non-great-making whether or not one has a favourite colour is that we cannot infer that a perfect being does have a favourite colour

[14] W. Mander, 'God and Personality', *Heythrop Journal* (1997), 38, 401–12, 403.

from the fact that He's perfect; not that we can infer that He does not. Here is a suggestion for an argument. Of logical necessity, a perfect being must either (a) have a favourite colour or (b) not have a favourite colour. Call the first the attribute of colour-favouritism; call the second the attribute of colour-indifferentism. If one insists that, as neither of these would be more great-making than the other, then a perfect being would have to have the attribute of colour-indifferentism, can one not fairly be accused of actually grading the attribute of colour-indifferentism as more great-making than the attribute of colour-favouritism, which – *ex hypothesi* – cannot be the case? Mander himself addresses the sort of view that I hold open as a possibility and says in effect that for God to have a favourite colour would be too 'arbitrary': 'In short, we may wonder, especially if we take God to be a necessary being, whether there can be anything arbitrary about him.'[15] But it is a logical necessity that there be something arbitrary about a perfect being if it is indeed a matter of value-indifference whether a being has the property of colour-favouritism or that of colour-indifferentism; if He has the property of colour-indifferentism, that is as arbitrary as if He has the property of colour-favouritism. If some of the properties that a perfect being may have are value-indifferent, then it's a logical necessity that there be arbitrariness of this sort in the most perfect being possible.[16]

The considerations sketched in the previous few paragraphs are to the effect that Perfect Being Theology alone will not enable us to decide between two or more sets of attributes the having of any one of which would make one such that none could be greater (and which have different great-making attributes among them) and between two or more sets of attributes the having of any one of which would make one such that none could be greater (and which have different non-great-making attributes among them). These considerations show the limits of Perfect Being Theology. These considerations do not, I suggest, show *weaknesses* in Perfect Being Theology. Perfect Being Theology alone will not allow us to know of all attributes whether or not

---

[15] 'God and Personality', 409.

[16] It's been suggested to me (by Martin Pickup) that perhaps colour indifferentism is less arbitrary, in that colour favouritism entails another arbitrary property, having a particular favourite colour, which colour indifferentism doesn't. If so and if having as little arbitrariness as possible is a great-making feature, colour indifferentism would then be ascribable, via Perfect Being Theology, to the greatest possible being. It may be then that this difference between Mander and me comes down to a difference in value judgement – I don't judge as great-making lack of arbitrariness (between options which don't differ in value); perhaps Mander does. This may be because I see this sort of arbitrariness as essential for being free when choosing between options which don't differ in value; see being free as great-making; and see it as necessary that there be options for an omnipotent being which don't differ in value. Perhaps Mander differs from me in one or more of these respects.

God has them, presuming He exists at all. But to say that one mode of argument can't tell you everything you might like to know about the nature of God is of course not to say that it can't tell you a lot.

To have characterised Perfect Being Theology with these few comments is to have sown dragon's teeth – a host of objections spring up, fully armed. Considerations of space mean that I can deal only with those which seem to me most pressing. There are three such.

First, we might consider the fact that the great-making status of many attributes is relative to the kind of thing in question. It's good for a bathroom mirror to be reflective (absent gerrymandered conditions), but it's neither good nor bad for a bathroom tile to be reflective (again, absent gerrymandered conditions). Are all great-making attributes like this – kind-relative? And, if so, do we not first need to decide what kind of thing God would be prior to being able to use Perfect Being Theology to consider candidate attributes as either great-making or not? The way through this issue is to deploy Perfect Being Theology on the attributes of being beings of certain kinds, the attribute of being a bathroom mirror, being a bathroom tile and so on. That is to say that we should ask of differing kinds of being if they're greater or less great than other kinds of being. Sometimes, assuredly, this question will not yield an answer for a given pair of kinds – are internal combustion engines greater or less great than sonatas? But sometimes this question will yield an answer. The case cogent to our concerns is, I suggest, this. Are *persons* greater than internal combustion engines; sonatas; bathroom mirrors; or indeed anything else? And it seems to me that this question yields the answer 'Yes', thus establishing that the greatest being possible will be a person. (Some theologians proceed further – 'beyond being' – or claim that God is not a being, but 'Being Itself', but such moves do not make sense.) Perfect Being Theology then is reflection on what the best person possible would be like.

Second, we might consider the fact that Perfect Being Theology rests on value judgements among other things. We're asking ourselves questions such as 'Are persons per se greater than sonatas per se?'; 'Is attribute A a great-making one for persons?'; 'Even if it is, would it be greater overall not to have it but instead to have attribute B, which is incompatible with A?'; and so on. And our value judgements are fallible. Leftow reports that as he gives perfect-being arguments, he has a 'nagging fear' that he is 'just making stuff up' as a result of the fact that 'our ideas of what it is to be perfect are inconsistent and flawed, and there is no guarantee that they match up with what God's perfection really is'.[17] I have the same nagging fear.

[17] B. Leftow, *God and Necessity* (Oxford: Oxford University Press, 2012), 12. He makes a similar point in 'Why Perfect Being Theology?', 111.

It is undoubtedly the case that one's value judgements are largely affected by one's culture. Nowadays, I can say that nobody reading this could have any doubts about the answer to the question, 'Which of these was the greater person – Churchill or Hitler?' But there were sane people in Germany (and beyond) in, let's say, 1936 (not perhaps exposed to all the evidence that was even then available, but sane nonetheless) who might have reversed the ranking that we so effortlessly provide. Is our culture even now blinding us to some facet of perfection and thus skewing our use of Perfect Being Theology? It may well be. And this prejudice may well be buried so deep within us that we cannot unearth, examine and repudiate it. As well as culture, there is the matter of individual temperament, which – in the case central to the concerns of this Element – seems to me more germane.

There are two broad ways of conceiving of God within the theistic tradition, the atemporalist way and the temporalist way. By the end of this Element, I'll thus have sketched two sets of what I will have maintained are logically possible divine attributes, those of the atemporal God and those of the temporal God. These sets overlap, but are not coextensive – the differing views of God's relations to time have knock-on effects for how omniscience, omnipotence and perfect goodness should be understood. And, by the end of the Element, I'll have offered a tentative assessment of the two views, my tentative assessment being that the atemporal God would be greater than the temporal and thus that this conception is to be preferred on the grounds of Perfect Being Theology. But whether or not my readers share that assessment will depend in part on their temperaments. As we'll see, the atemporal God strikes some people as austere, detached, lifeless, whereas the temporal God strikes them as more genial, involved and responsive; and, having thus been struck, temperamentally they warm more to the second conception than to the first. The point of view to which such people are led naturally inclines them to invert the ranking of greatness that I endorse and it is a point of view from which they cannot be dislodged by argument alone.

The dependence of Perfect Being Theology on value judgements and these on our cultures and individual temperaments is then, I concede, 'an issue', but it is hardly one unique to Perfect Being Theology. The same issue arises in moral and political philosophy. Arguably the issue arises in philosophy per se, as there are values presupposed in argument per se – e.g. that it's bad to be inconsistent. Thus, judgements of value are needed however value-free the subject matter of the arguments we're considering. The best we can do is – as always because as of necessity – our best. We can't let the fact that our best may well not be good enough (and may not be good enough in part because we haven't got a good enough conception of what it would be to be good enough) undermine our resolve.

Third, we might consider the fact that Perfect Being Theology rests on judgements of possibility, among other things. Leftow goes on from the passage just cited to point this out too. 'Our intuitions about absolute possibility, again, probably are not wholly reliable; probably we sometimes take as absolutely possible what is merely epistemically possible.'[18] So, to return to the issue of adjudicating between the atemporal God and the temporal God: it's very plausible that at most one of the atemporal God and the temporal God is metaphysically possible. Given that, the temporalist may say that, even if things along the line I shall endeavour to show were to be shown, viz. that, in various ways, the atemporal God would be greater than the temporal, so what? Perfect Being Theology tells us God is the best being *possible* and the atemporal God fails of the relevant sort of possibility. The same sort of point may be made, *mutatis mutandis*, by the person who favours the atemporal conception of God should the proponent of the temporal God maintain that his or her God would be greater.

Now, I have argued elsewhere that we can compare metaphysical impossibilities with metaphysical possibilities and reach some non-trivially-true evaluative beliefs about them.[19] But this is a vexed issue and in this context I must just assume it. For my part, then, both the atemporal God and the temporal God are logical possibilities. And the methodology of Perfect Being Theology as I am taking it suggests we should compare any logically possible plausible candidate for being the best possible being to see which, if any, is most deserving of the name 'God'; thus, these two conceptions of God – the atemporal and the temporal – are the ones to compare. When I do so compare them, I find – tentatively (aware as I am that some 'temperamental' bias must always play a role in such a grading) – that the atemporal God would be greater were He to exist than the temporal God. If you accept Perfect Being Theology thus understood but disagree with my conclusion, you can either maintain that the atemporal God is a logical impossibility; or that I'm just wrong in my value judgement that the atemporal God as I conceptualise Him would be greater than the temporal God as I conceptualise Him; or that my own ways of making best sense of the atemporalist and/or temporalist conceptualisations are not up to the task. Most theists who agree on my Perfect-Being-Theology starting point, but disagree on where we should end up, will take the second and/or third of these paths, but, in any case, we'll be back to the limitations that I have just discussed, limitations again, let me stress, not in the method of Perfect Being Theology but in us as we try our best to transcend our cultures and temperaments and use that

---

[18] Leftow, God and Necessity, 12.

[19] See, e.g., T. J. Mawson, 'Doing Natural Theology Consistently', *Religious Studies* (2017), 53 (3), 339–52.

method. Again then, the best we can do is our best – our best to judge of values and possibilities; to note our fallibility about such judgements; and to proceed accordingly, with resolve but also with humility.

So, my approach will be that of Perfect Being Theology thus understood. But behind the method of Perfect Being Theology as I am conceiving it, there is another 'regulative' idea, one different from the one on which I have been concentrating so far in my exposition. So far, I have been concentrating on Perfect Being Theology's injunction that we conceive of God as the best being possible. That idea obviously has much to recommend it to the theist. Not least, it is attractive to him or her in that it forearms to an extent against atheistic arguments proceeding from alleged incoherencies within some of the divine attributes or incompatibilities between them. 'Could an omnipotent being create an object so heavy that He Himself couldn't then lift it?' the atheist might pointedly ask. And, however the theist responds, some pressure is put on (at least some understandings of) omnipotence. 'Surely an omnipotent being, however omnipotence may sensibly be defined, would have to be able to do evil and yet – equally surely – a being who was of necessity perfectly good would have to be unable to do evil; and thus no being can be both' the atheist might continue, again calling for a response. The idea that we should think of God as the best being possible promises to dissipate the force of such lines of argument. It promises to give general licence to the following type of response. 'Nothing of this sort can show that God – understood as the best being possible – doesn't exist; it can only, at worst, show that the best being possible isn't as some theists have rashly described Him; He isn't – for example – omnipotent under the relevant understanding; or He isn't of necessity perfectly good (rather than contingently perfectly good); or what have you.' And we'll see this dissipation of some of the traditional puzzles surrounding the divine attributes as the Element plays out. But there is another regulative idea behind Perfect Being Theology, one that stops this being a 'catch-all' solution to problems of this sort, viz. the idea that to be worthy of the name 'God', the being in question has to be, well, *perfect*.

In practising Perfect Being Theology, we're not practising 'Pretty-Good Being Theology' or even – slightly more grandly – 'Maximally Good Being Theology'.[20] If it were shown that the best being possible could only have

---

[20] The first term is suggested to me by Leftow, God and Necessity; the second, by Nagasawa (Y. Nagasawa, 'A New Defence of Anselmian Theism', *Philosophical Quarterly* (2008), 58(233), 577–96) who is a keen exponent of this dissipating strategy. See also his *Maximal God* (Oxford: Oxford University Press, 2017).

enough power to create a universe like ours; would have to be largely ignorant; could only be about as morally worthy as the average human; and so on, then the theist might still say that something god-like, possibly even a god (without the capital 'G'), could nevertheless exist. But he or she would surely need to concede that it had been show that the God in whom he or she had previously believed could not, after all, exist.[21] That seems right to me. Theism is committed not simply to the best being possible existing, but to the best being possible being perfect. There may be *some* 'well, I suppose I meant as perfect as possible' wriggle room here for the theist, but the very word 'perfect' sets limits to such room and sets these limits quite narrowly. If 'as perfect as possible' were to be shown to fall below a no-doubt-vague, but also no-doubt-high threshold, then theism would be refuted.

One might think from this that another way of settling the issue between the atemporalist and temporalist conceptions of God would present itself. I have said that I'll argue that an atemporal God would be greater than a temporal one. Perhaps, then, one might think, the best temporal god (note the small 'g', the use of which already suggests the position to be articulated) can plausibly be presented as falling below the relevant threshold: if that sort of god were the best being metaphysically possible, then the best being metaphysically possible wouldn't be perfect and thus wouldn't be worthy of the name 'God'. So, if there is to be a God, He must be as the atemporalist conceptualises Him. A case can be made for such a claim; I shall press it; and I shall press it as far as I think I can in good conscience (and consciousness of its weaknesses) press it. But I shall argue that in the end it is insufficient. There is enough 'well, I suppose I meant as perfect as possible' wriggle room for the temporal God to survive, even if – I hope to show – uncomfortably. So, all I can promise is that the disputes among theists will continue. (And nobody can doubt that the disputes between theists and those who disagree with theism will continue.) The disputes will continue, but let us start with what it is all theists agree about.

---

[21] Issues in the philosophy of language intrude here. On some understandings of how proper names work (assuming 'God' is in fact best understood as a proper name), even if there exists a being who is well above any plausible 'threshold' for counting as the God of theism, if that being hasn't in fact interrelated with history so as to found any religions, He isn't actually the referent of the name 'God' as adherents of any of the world's religions use the term. And if some merely god-like being (a highly advanced extraterrestrial lifeform, say) actually led the Jews out of Egypt; incarnated himself in Jesus; or what have you (one would have to tweak the account in various religion-specific ways), then, given how the name 'God' was introduced, that being gets to be the referent of 'God' even though he falls well below any plausible threshold for counting as a perfect being.

1 A Transcendent, Immanent, Eternal Person

Personhood

I start with the divine attribute of personhood – the property of being a person.[22] In part, I start here because it is in its commitment to the fundamental supernatural reality being personal, rather than impersonal, that the Western religions divide from the Eastern. I say this, but I must concede immediately that this division is by no means clear-cut. There are theistic versions of Hinduism, for example, which place their personal gods, Śiva or Viṣṇu, beyond the otherwise-ineluctable mechanics of karma, as well as those which place their gods under the rule of what is then seen as the more ultimate spiritual karmic law. And, in the West, Greek polytheism – though (oddly) never worked through with as much philosophical rigour as it might have been – seems to posit that its personal gods, Zeus and the like, are subject to supernatural constraints not of their own creation (and sometimes even natural constraints); Stoic metaphysics (which one might maintain is a religion) seems to see ultimate supernatural reality as an impersonal mechanism, beyond our capacities to affect to any extent. And then we have what are sometimes called 'magical' religions, those which treat the ultimate supernatural reality as an impersonal mechanism, but one which may be manipulated to some extent by those who know the right magic. In addition, in the West, we have a small number of recent theologians who have wished to place themselves within the Christian tradition, yet have denied that God is a person, seeing the theistic model discussed in this Element as something to be 'transcended'. Be all that as it may, the personhood of God is in fact presupposed in all the stories that the main religions of the West – Judaism, Christianity and Islam – tell of human-kind's encounter with ultimate reality. According to Judaism and Christianity, for example, 'The Lord spoke to Moses face to face, as a man speaks to his friend.'[23] According to Islam, 'God said: "O Mankind! Be dutiful to your Lord, Who created you from a single person [Adam] and from him [Adam] He created his wife [Eve], and from them both He created many men and women".'[24] The common presumption behind these and the multitude of other stories that these religions tell of God's relations with humanity is that God is a person. He is an agent. He has beliefs. He cares about things. He is thus pleased (and sometimes displeased) by the actions of others. And He Himself performs actions, most primordially His action in creating the world, but also

---

[22] Here and hereafter (except in discussing the divine property of unity), I sweep to one side complications that are introduced by the Doctrine of the Trinity, according to which God is not *a* person, but three persons.
[23] Exodus 33:11.   [24] Surah 4:1.

on theism (in contrast to deism) He continues to interact with His creation – most particularly us – by speaking to prophets and indeed, in a less dramatic way, to many others, guiding us in response to prayer. On theism, then, the most ultimate supernatural reality is personal. The alternative religious view – which, as I say, one may think of as more typical of the religions of the East – sees the ultimate supernatural reality as an impersonal force, a karmic mechanism, which may be the explanation of the events we observe, but which does not bring them about by actions which it is choosing to perform. It doesn't believe. It doesn't care. It's neither pleased, nor displeased by what we do. It doesn't listen to our prayers or respond to them. It just impersonally works on us and everything else.

Whole books have been written about what it is that makes a person a person, and, while there is diversity of opinion, some common elements emerge when people reflect on the attributes essential to personhood. Persons essentially display rationality; they have beliefs; they are loci of moral respect; they show respect for others; they are sentient; they are conscious; they are self-conscious; they have a psychic unity; they act; they communicate to others. Despite saying that persons essentially display these attributes, accounts which bring these (and other) attributes together as constitutive of what it is to be a person are at their most plausible when they allow that persons may fail to have at least some of these attributes, at least to an extent (after all, many of them are degreed attributes) and/or at least for a time, yet remain persons nonetheless. But, equally, it is very plausible that to the extent that a given candidate for personhood failed to show these characteristics at all (or, if he or she once had them, started failing to show them over a protracted period), that would conceptually undermine his or her status as a person (or as a continuing person) and thus is generated the plausibility of these attributes being of the essence of personhood.

Compare Mander, who says that, 'being a person is an all or nothing affair, not a matter of degree'.[25] Mander is at this stage endorsing what he takes to be Nagel's view of what it is to be a person, namely (according to Mander) that there is something that it is like to be that thing (phenomenologically, from the inside). This is an odd view of the nature of personhood to attribute to Nagel, as he is most famous in this context for reflecting sympathetically on the thought that a bat (which I take it is not a person according to Nagel) has, in the nature of its experience, something that it's like to be the thing it is, viz. a bat. Hence, the famous title of his piece, 'What Is It Like to Be a Bat?'.[26] So, it seems to me,

---

[25] 'God and Personality', 402.

[26] T. Nagel, 'What Is It Like to Be a Bat?', *Philosophical Review* (1974), 83(4) 435–50.

Nagel doesn't take having something that it is like to be the thing that one is as sufficient for personhood. There's much plausibility in its being necessary, admittedly. But even if a necessary condition of personhood is that there be something that it's like (to be a person) and that is an undegreed attribute, it doesn't follow – given that there may be other attributes that are degreed and work in the manner I sketch – that personhood is not degreed. It's a necessary condition of being a tall policeman that one be a policeman, and being a policeman is perhaps an undegreed property. One either is or one isn't a policeman. But tallness is a degreed attribute. So, I disagree with Mander's argument, as he goes on thus, 'There either is or there isn't something that it is like to be a given creature. You either are or you aren't a person.' Even if whether or not one is a person is a determinate matter – perhaps there is some determinate threshold for this cluster of properties or a proper subset of it and one either passes this threshold or one doesn't – one could still maintain as I do that, given that some will clear this threshold (be it determinate or not) by greater margins than others, we may speak of those who clear the threshold by greater margins as more persons or as better at being persons than those who clear it by lesser margins. The situation might be analogous to the following. Consider a continuum of cases of people sitting at pianos and depressing their keys. At one extreme, they bang keys randomly; perhaps they are a very young child trying to play music, having watched an adult do so, but they have no idea how to do this and no significant coordination anyway. They determinately fail to play music. At the other extreme, the person is a concert pianist, playing – say – something by Mozart. In between, there is a continuum of cases. We can say that past a certain point up this continuum, the person in question would definitely be playing music, but what they would be playing higher up would be even more musical, even better. Among those who are musical, some are more musical than others; some are better musicians than others.

Many of the attributes constitutive of personhood are then degreed. Thus, using the recipe of Perfect Being Theology, we should consider of each of the degreed attributes whether they're 'more is better' attributes. Suppose one is clearly above whatever threshold there might be with respect to this cluster of properties to count as a person; if one then considers a degreed attribute, is it plausibly the case that the more of it one has, the better one is as a person? Many of these attributes can easily be seen in this way to be 'more is better' attributes. When it comes to rationality, for example, we observe that we human persons are rational, but only to an extent and only some of the time; sometimes our powers fail us. And of course some people suffer such disintegration of their rationality through mental illness that we find it hard to interpret their utterances as speech or their bodily movements as actions at all. Be that as it may and however rational we may be, we can agree that if we were more rational, we'd be better. Rationality is a 'more is better' attribute. A perfect person then would not be limited at all in this respect; He would be supremely rational. And what of the beliefs that our rationality orders? Even when they are rightly ordered, our beliefs are a mixed (and small) bag. We human persons believe things about many topics, but some of our true beliefs fall short of knowledge (they're just luckily true); some of our beliefs fail even to be true; and of some topics we remain entirely and unthinkingly ignorant. And that's just for those of us in moderate health. Again, severe mental illness – dementia for example – can rob people of so much of what they had previously known through memory and of their general knowledge about how the world works and thus deprive them of mental content to express, that, while their bodies remain, the people they once were can seem to disappear entirely. Be that as it may and again however many beliefs that count as knowledge we might manage to have, a perfect person would obviously not be at all limited in this respect; He'd have beliefs about all topics and they'd all be infallibly true; He'd be omniscient. If we turn to consider how we humans interact with one another, we may observe that we manage to show one another the respect that is our due at least some of the time, but by no means always. We – all of us, not just the Adolf Hitlers of this world – sometimes wilfully do to other people what we know they have the right not to have done to them. And when we do so fail, even if not falling so far short of the standards required for us that we cease to be persons, we thereby fail to be as good at being persons as we could have been; we let ourselves down. And some do fall even further than most of us. Again, some extreme mental illnesses – in this case a certain type of psychopathy – show us those who are so adversely affected in this domain that we may be tempted to fail to count them as persons at all. Again, be that as it may, we can see that a perfect person would not be at all like this; He would be perfectly good. So, in sum, if there is a God, then He is not just a person, but, through His having the degreed properties criterial of personhood to the maximal extent (as well as having the undegreed ones), He is more of a person than any of us can ever aspire to be.

Transcendence

Being the most perfect person possible has direct implications for God's relations to other supernatural stuff (if there is any) and any natural stuff (and of course we know there is some of this). In particular, a perfect person cannot depend on anything for His existence. And, as He exists as the thing He most fundamentally is (the most perfect person possible) in virtue of His possessing His essential attributes, so this entails that He cannot depend on anything for His essential attributes. He must thus be ontologically distinct from the universe He chose to create; He could annihilate it at any moment and not thereby cease to exist. And if the universe affects God (and we will want to say that it does), it can only do so by affecting His accidental attributes. This independence from anything other than Himself for His essential attributes is the attribute of transcendence and seeing God as transcendent of the universe in this sense demarcates theism from pantheism, which identifies God with the universe.

From what has been said so far, divine transcendence might seem to be a relational attribute – if *a* is to transcend, then surely there must be a *b* for it to transcend – and so one might perhaps wonder if divine transcendence cannot in fact be an essential property of God. If there had not been anything other than God, there'd have been no *b* for Him to relate to in the way it characterises (God doesn't transcend Himself); it was a possibility that there be nothing other than God prior to God's choice to create; and yet, had God failed to create, He'd still have existed. In fact, this is not a problem. Transcendence as characterised is independence (in one's existence and thus essential attributes) from things other than oneself and a being could be perfectly transcendent in this sense – independent of *everything* other than itself in respect of its existence and essential attributes – even if there were nothing other than itself; indeed, in such a case, its perfect transcendence would trivially follow from the fact that there was nothing other than itself. In other words, for *a* to transcend, it is not necessary that there exist a *b* (distinct from *a*) such that *a* is independent of *b*; it is only necessary that there does not exist a *b* (distinct from *a*) such that *a* is dependent on *b*.

God then is essentially perfectly transcendent, but we can see that we are what we might thus call 'imperfectly transcendent'. As well as there being bits of matter on which we do depend for our continuing existence or essential attributes, there are also bits of matter on which we do not depend. We hear about a hurricane affecting a distant island and killing several people there; we are not essentially affected, though – if we are sympathetic – we are accidentally affected; we feel sorry for the victims. Indeed, there are vast sections of our universe, beyond our light cone, that *cannot* affect us at all (absent supernatural mediation).

This last example might lead us to reflect that one way in which a given *a* can transcend a given *b* is by having *nothing at all* to do with it. So, if God were to have created another universe, with different matter and different laws, and if He were to have done so in a way that had nothing to do with us and it and its denizens had always been and will always remain causally unreachable by any of us and we unreachable by any of them, then we human persons would transcend that universe as completely as God would transcend it. There would still be this difference between us and God in respect of transcendence: it would not be of necessity that we perfectly transcended it, whereas it would be of necessity that God do so. Be that as it may, that's not the relation – or, rather, absence of a relation – that God has to the created order according to theism. God may transcend, perfectly transcend indeed, but He does so not by having nothing at all to do with anything; rather, He is more closely involved with everything than anyone else. 'Is involved', not just 'was involved', at the moment of creation (distinguishing theism from deism). This is another attribute of His then. Sometimes, this attribute is called 'omnipresence', but on stylistic grounds alone (to pair with transcendence), I prefer the word 'immanence'.

Immanence

While God is ontologically distinct from the universe in the way that the attribute of transcendence characterises, He nevertheless is, as the ancients put it, that in which we live, move and have our being. This is the divine attribute of immanence and it is, I contend, best understood as God's knowing everything about anything other than God directly (that is without needing to work it out from something already known) and His being able to affect anything other than God directly (without needing first to affect something else). So, God's being immanent at the centre of our sun, for example, is, first, God's knowing what is happening there, not by working out what must be happening there given His knowledge of the laws of nature and the phenomena that He observes happening farther out; He doesn't have to work it out; He knows it directly. And, second, it is its being true of the centre of the sun that were God to want to produce some effect there, He wouldn't have to do it by first producing an effect farther out and using some mechanism to carry that influence into the centre; He could produce that effect directly in the centre.

Again, one might worry about the status of immanence as an essential property – if a is to be immanent, must there not be some b (other than a) in which it is immanent? And was it not a possibility that God not have created anything, in which case there would have been no such b and yet He still have existed? A terminological clarification shows this worry to be misguided – it is one parallel to the one deployed in fine-tuning the notion of transcendence. A being, a, is perfectly immanent if there is nothing of which it does not know directly or cannot control directly. Again, for *a* to be perfectly immanent, it is not necessary that there be some *b* non-identical to *a*, such that *a* can know about that *b* directly and can control that *b* directly, just that there be no *b* such that *a* either cannot know about it directly or cannot control it directly. Thus, in that possible world where God exists yet fails to create anything, God remains as perfectly immanent as He remains perfectly transcendent.

We have seen that only God can be perfectly transcendent, but we can be imperfectly so. Similarly, only God can be perfectly immanent, but we can be imperfectly immanent; as well as there being bits of the universe that we cannot know about directly and cannot control directly, there are bits of the universe which we do know about directly and which we do control directly. We call bits of the universe to which we have this relation our bodies (or at least parts of them). Or so I shall maintain. My doing so depends on my rendering plausible the direct-knowledge and direct-control conditions as two conditions which are jointly sufficient for something to be a part of one's body. With this aim, I'll illustrate the view now.

So, rest your right hand palm-down on the nearest flat hard surface, a tabletop or some such; push down with your hand on that surface. Assuming, as I am, that you have a normally functioning right hand (that it is not anaesthetised or paralysed), it meets the following two conditions. First, you are able to learn about what is going on in that hand directly, without first needing to learn something else. You can just feel of your hand that it is subject to an upwards force (the one corresponding to the force you are pushing it down with); if the surface is a cold one, you just know that your hand is getting cold; and so on. Second, you can affect this hand directly, without first needing consciously to affect something else. When you followed my instruction to push down, you didn't first need to perform some more basic action. Were your hand to have been anaesthetised, you would have needed to look at where it was to learn about it. Were your hand to have been paralysed, you would have needed to use your other hand (assuming it was not similarly paralysed) to follow my instructions, getting the paralysed hand into position and pushing down by using the non-paralysed one to manipulate it. As it is though, you know about and are able to control this hand directly and, I maintain, these two conditions together are sufficient for this hand to be a part of your body. (NB: I do not argue that they are necessary, just jointly sufficient; there are bits of our bodies that do not satisfy either of these conditions.)

Theists have tended to speak of God's incorporeality, His not having a body. But, for myself, I have argued at greater length elsewhere for the view that I have just sketched – that it is a sufficient condition of someone's having a section of matter (or indeed, more broadly, a section of space – whether it be occupied by matter or not) be a part of his or her body that he or she can know about the state of that section of matter directly and can control it directly, that he or she is immanent in it as I have defined immanence.[27] If I am right in that, then it would be a necessary condition of God's being truly incorporeal that He could not do this for any section of matter. But, as we have just seen, according to theism, while God is transcendent, He is also immanent; while He is not subject to the limitations of the physical universe, He fully pervades it with His mind, knowing and being able to act directly at all places and times. So, for myself, I conclude that we should say that our universe as a whole is a part of God's body; if there are other universes, then ours is a proper part of His body; if not, then it's the whole of it. God does not have the attribute of incorporeality.

It is only fair to stress that not many theists agree with me.

There are a number of objections to my view, most of which rely on adding necessary conditions for embodiment to my picture, conditions which it's plausible to maintain God wouldn't meet. For example, one might insist that for genuine embodiment, one must in some way (that transcendence rules out) depend on the matter in which one is embodied. One might insist that to have a body is to be spatially related to something else and, as the universe itself is not spatially related to anything else, it cannot be anyone's body. And so on. These sorts of objection would have to be dealt with on a case-by-case basis and I must – rather weakly – plead considerations of space as all that prevents me from doing so adequately here. In any case, I won't engage with my opponents on this front. But, in a spirit of being charitable to my opponents, let me sketch out what I myself think is the most promising area from which a counterattack to my view might be launched.

On my view, various things count as parts of our bodies that it is counter-intuitive so to count. Let me give one example, though examples can be multiplied and indeed it is in their multiplication that the force of this counter-argument lies. If we are experienced drivers, we will sometimes have such a relationship to our cars that, on my account, they will temporarily become parts of our bodies. We will feel directly – say – that the steering is pulling to the left (thereby learning about a section of matter directly); we will instinctively compensate (without first needing consciously to do something else); and so on. One needs to finesse the example a bit, but I would concede that for certain periods, on my view, if one is a proficient driver, one's car (or bits of it) become a part of one's body. And some will take this sort of implication as a *reductio* of my overly casual, as they will think of it, attitude towards direct-knowledge and

---

[27] T. J. Mawson, 'God's Body', *Heythrop Journal* (2006), 47, 171–81.

direct-control as conditions jointly sufficient for body ownership. My response?

Dennett famously defines what it is to 'outsmart' one's opponent as to accept as obviously true the conclusion of their *reductio* of one's position. In the end, my response to counterarguments of the sort just sketched is a weak outsmarting one. I say 'weak', as I would agree with the proponents of these sorts of counterarguments that it's not obviously true that cars (and the like) can become parts of our bodies, but, on balance, I'm inclined to accept that it's non-obviously true and resist the characterisation of such lines of argument as *reductio*s accordingly. There is a movement in the philosophy of mind called 'Extended Mind', where one is encouraged to think of people as, for example, knowing things even if they need to use things exterior to the body (as it would ordinarily be taken) – e.g. their mobile telephones – to retrieve the information in question. So, for example, if Rodes is someone who is such that if he were asked if he knew Lindy's new number would effortlessly and unthinkingly look it up on his ever-present telephone, we should say of Rodes that he knows Lindy's new number. That would be the 'Extended Mind' approach: what we know needn't all be 'in the head'; our minds can extend beyond our skins. Well, that may seem odd, but my view – which may indeed take some of the oddness out of Extended Mind views – could be characterised as an 'Extended Body' view; the body needn't all be 'in the skin'.

I would agree then that the view just sketched is not intuitively plausible, 'straight out of the gate' as it were. Thus, it is perhaps worth pointing out that, despite my having belaboured the point somewhat, not much turns on whether or not I am right in all of this. If I am right, we may talk about the universe as literally God's body; if I am wrong, God may in fact be described as literally incorporeal, but we may talk of Him as having a relationship to the universe that is closely analogous to that which we have towards our bodies.

To return to common ground: God is a transcendent, yet immanent person; if He creates something other than Himself, He will be perfectly transcendent of it yet immanent in it. We know He did in fact create something other than Himself, a spatiotemporal system that we call the universe; so, He is perfectly transcendent of, yet immanent in, that. Thus far we have been considering God's transcending yet being immanent in space and things in space (e.g. bits of matter), but what about time? Time is something other than God; must God not transcend and be immanent in that? Here we come to the great divide among those who hold to the theistic concept of God. According to the atemporalists, God does fully transcend time in the sense introduced earlier. According to the temporalists, He does not; were it to cease to exist, He would cease to exist. Temporalists may say that the universe's time is nested within

another time – God's time or 'metaphysical' time – and, if so, then they may say
that God transcends the universe's time, but they cannot say that He transcends
this second sort of time. Of course, if the time in which God essentially exists
(which He fails to transcend) is uncreated (as it must be), then it is very
plausibly metaphysically necessary that it exist; it thus can no more cease to
exist than God can on any account and thus the 'if-it-did-cease-to-exist-so-
would-God' implication is not merely a counterfactual, but a counter-possible.
And the temporalist may say that, as perfect transcendence only requires
independence in one's existence and essential attributes from things other
than oneself, it only remains for him or her to eschew counting the most
ultimate time as a thing for him or her to be able to say of his or her God that
He is fully transcendent of everything. Certainly, time is only dubiously a
substantial thing and it would be failing to transcend a substantial thing that
would be the real 'hit' to a being's greatness. Still, we see here the first opening
of a gap between the atemporalist and the temporalist conceptions of God, a gap
which will widen yet further, the gap that gives people of different temperaments reason to prefer one conception of God over the other, gives people with
my temperament reason to think the atemporal God would be greater than the
temporal.

Eternality

There are two broad views that one may take about the ontology of time.
Presentism is the view that the present moment, the now, is the only moment of
time that exists. The past no longer exists; the future has yet to exist. Eternalism is
the view that past, present and future equally exist. Temporalists tend to affirm
presentism and atemporalists tend to affirm eternalism. As my argument unfolds,
we shall see how commitments on the ontology of time shape each side's views of
God's knowledge, power and goodness.[28]

All theists agree then that God exists without beginning or end in time,
but some – the atemporalists – say that He also exists without succession;

---

[28] I shall try – as far as is possible – not to assume anything about which theory of time is to be
preferred, but one's ontology of time does affect in which direction one is then reasonable in
running various arguments. For example, on eternalism, as every moment of time equally exists,
so they are all in a sense 'there' for God to know about (potentially), though, if He exists only at
a particular moment in time, the now, then, for reasons given in due course, He will have
difficulty knowing infallibly what will be happening at those moments which are currently
future. On presentism, arguably an atemporal God cannot know which moment is now, for that
is, arguably, something that can only be known by someone who exists now. And perhaps
ignorance of an infinite number of tensed facts springs from this one source. I do tend to
eternalism myself, on grounds that lie well outside the philosophy of religion, and that
preference no doubt affects my treatment of the issues. This Element's subject is not the
philosophy of time, so all I can do is draw attention to those effects as I go along.

others – the temporalists – say that He exists with succession. There are various ways of understanding eternality within each of these two, atemporalist and temporalist, camps. And there are some views that seek to straddle the divide – God is atemporal without creation, but temporal with it. Considerations of space mean that I can only discuss what are to my mind the most plausible variants of the atemporalist and temporalist models. Henceforth, then, when I refer to the atemporalist view and temporalist view, I shall have in mind only what I believe to be the most plausible variants of those views unless I say otherwise.

To bring out the difference between atemporalism and temporalism as I am understanding them, let us suppose that the only thing other than God that exists is this universe and that it began with the Big Bang some fourteen billion years ago and has been expanding since then, being now a large (but finite) size; and, let us further suppose that, at some stage in the future, either due to a big crunch or as a result of God simply deciding that 'enough is enough' and bringing it all to a close (the eschaton), the universe will cease to exist. On such a hypothesis, according to the atemporalist view, God did not exist before the Big Bang; there was no 'before the Big Bang', because time came into existence with the Big Bang; and, when the universe ceases to exist, God will not be there afterwards; there will be no 'after the universe'.[29] There can be no time which is a time 'before time began' and no time which is a time 'after time has ended' and the Big Bang and big crunch/eschaton mark the beginning and end of time. According to the temporalists, by contrast, time is bigger than the *ex hypothesi* finite amount of it that has been and will be occupied by the history of the universe; God existed in it before the universe did and He will exist in it after the universe has ceased to do so. According to the atemporalist, then, God's relation to time parallels His relation to space. Not so for the temporalist. According to the temporalist, God's relation to time is quite different from His relation to space.

I have just argued that it is sufficient for one's being at a particular space that one knows what is going on there directly and can act there directly. It seems to me that we should make the parallel claim about time; it is sufficient for one's

---

[29] Some caution is needed here as if God destroys the universe but immediately transfers any people still around to some temporally extended afterlife, then this afterlife could be described as temporally posterior to the universe (or at least this section of it could be so described (perhaps such an afterlife is already 'up and running' and its residents are being constantly added to by transfers from this universe; it thus overlaps, in its earlier parts, the universe)). On such a model, the afterlife is temporally, but not spatially, related to the universe. I do not wish to suggest this is the best model for thinking of the afterlife, only with this note to make sure that even if I may seem to rule it out as I do my best to characterise the atemporalist's understanding of divine eternality on which I am focusing, I do so merely so as not to raise complications that are needless in that context.

being at a particular time that one knows what is going on then directly and that one can act then directly. It would follow that if there is a perfectly immanent God, then He exists at all times; of all times it is true that He knows what is happening then directly and can act then directly. Can the atemporalist in consistency say this? If not, then it may be that what the temporalist 'loses', relative to the atemporalist, with respect to not being able to affirm transcendence of time, he or she gains back with respect to immanence, in being able to affirm that while the atemporalist may not. In fact, though, it seems to me that the atemporalist can consistently affirm full immanence and endorse my account of direct knowledge and direct control as sufficient to be at any time one exercises them. The atemporal God is at every time, just as He is at every space; but He manages to be so without being within time or within space. I use 'within' to imply that a thing is bounded by a space/time which exists outside it, and 'at' to void that implication. So, for example, I would say that this universe (if there is no other) exists at all spaces but not within space and, if there is no time outside it, it exists at all times and not within time too. But if I am right in that, then there is at least one downside. It is not that we can distinguish the atemporalist view from the temporalist view by saying that which it might perhaps first occur to us to say, that according to the atemporalist, God exists, yet exists at *no* times, whereas according to the temporalist, He exists and exists at *all* times (and time is everlasting in both forwards and backwards directions). Perhaps, then, reasonably wishing to avoid this downside, one might hope that I'm not right. As we saw in discussing my views on body ownership and the like, I may be regarded as too lax in my understanding of what is sufficient for existence at a place; similarly, I may be regarded as too lax (or as in some other way erring) in my understanding of what it sufficient for existing at a time. If it is right so to regard me, then one may perhaps distinguish atemporalism from temporalism in the manner just sketched: the atemporalist says that God exists but exists at no times; the temporalist, that God exists at all times (and time is everlasting in the forwards and backwards directions). Of course, if I am wrong about the sufficiency of direct knowledge and direct control for being at a time, it only follows that God's immanence in time is not best understood by the atemporalist as His being at all times in exactly the same sense that we are at whatever time it happens to be for us now; the word 'at' in the case of God would be being used somewhat analogously to its normal use were one to say that the atemporal God is 'at' all times. Again, then, despite my having belaboured the point somewhat, not much turns on whether or not I'm right. Still, as I think I am right, allow me to sketch a few other ways of characterising the difference between the atemporalist and the temporalist, ways which avoid these issues.

The simplest way is to revert to the difference between the atemporalist and the temporalist when it comes to transcendence. The atemporalist says that God transcends time; the temporalist, that He does not. Or one might consider the notion of succession; the atemporalist and temporalist both say that God is without beginning or end; the atemporalist adds that He is also without succession, whereas the temporalist says that He exists with succession. Or one could consider the matter counterfactually: the atemporalist asserts that if God had not created a universe, there would have been no time (or at least need not have been time (He might have created something else temporal)), whereas the temporalist believes that even if God had not created a universe, there would still have had to have been time.[30] According to the atemporalist, there is no time within which the created order exists; by contrast, according to the temporalist, there *is* time within which it exists – God's time, if you will ('metaphysical time', if you prefer).

Mullins is unconvinced, saying that 'If God exists at any time, He must be temporal ... Mawson claims, like Anselm, that existing at every time is not sufficient for existing in time ... I do not find this distinction obvious. I dare say it is empty ... the timeless God under consideration here exists at every time and thus has temporal location. That is sufficient for God to be temporal.'[31] I hope that what I have said will have spoken to Mullins's concerns. God exists at every time in the sense that He is immanent at every time (He can know about it and act at it directly), but not 'in' (I tend to use the word 'within') time. Indeed, God transcends time (as He transcends space) in the manner specified – He is not dependent on it for His existence and essential properties (as He is on temporalism). As to the notion of location, one would of course be helped by a definition, but it seems to me that one may say that an object's having a location is to be understood as its occupying some *particular* position within space, such that, by being there, it fails to be somewhere else. If so understood, then everything in the universe has a location, but the universe itself does not; and, again, nor does God in virtue of His perfect immanence, i.e. omnipresence – there's nowhere where He's not. On other understandings of location, it might

---

[30] Here then I disagree with Mullins, who says that this way of characterising the difference between the atemporal and the temporal God will not work as 'divine simplicity forces the atemporalist to say that this is the only possible world. If this is right, there is no possible world where God exists without the temporal universe' (R. T. Mullins, *The End of the Timeless God* ((Oxford: Oxford University Press, 2016), 150). I do not endorse an understanding of the attribute of simplicity which results in saying that this is the only possible world; there are metaphysically possible worlds where God exists without any temporal created being, viz. those worlds where He chooses not to create any temporal being, e.g. no universes. On the atemporalist understanding, in those worlds time does not exist. On the temporalist understanding, in those worlds time still exists.

[31] *End of the Timeless God*, 149–53.

follow on my account that one should say that God is located everywhere, in which case He would be an instance of what is sometimes called an extended simple. I myself, with my minority opinion about what is sufficient for body ownership and inclination to say that people are at where their bodies are at (and that it's sufficient to be at a time that one can directly know about and directly affect things at it), would say that God is at every space–time, even though, with my view that persons can be at places and times where they have no parts (human persons are uniformly where and when their bodies are, but their bodies are not parts of them), I would say that that does not mean God has any spatial or temporal parts.

Atemporalism and temporalism as just sketched seem then to me the two views that one might most reasonably hold on the issue of God's relation to time.

On atemporalism, God perfectly transcends time; He exists without beginning, end or succession. If I am right in my minority view about what is sufficient nevertheless to be said truly to exist at a time, viz. that one be immanent at that time in the sense defined (able to know about it and affect it directly), then God nevertheless can truly be said to be at all times. If I am wrong in thinking that a being's having immanence at a time is sufficient for the being to be at that time, then God is not strictly at any time; He can of course still be said to be analogously 'at' every time. In either case, then, the fact of His immanence remains; it's just a question of whether or not my 'at' locution is misjudged (when intended literally rather than merely analogically). God is not within time, even if He is (as I would maintain) at all times. Some find it odd to say of something that it both exists at times and yet does not exist within time. And of course nothing we come across in our day-to-day lives – other humans, tables and chairs – fails to have both properties or neither (abstracta), but the universe exists at all times, but not within time, according to the atemporalist, just as it exists at all spaces but not within space, according to everyone.[32]

On temporalism, God does not perfectly transcend time per se – though with the distinction between uncreated time and created time, He may be said to

---

[32] Of course, on the temporalist model, the universe too is within God's time (metaphysical time, if you will); nothing ever manages to exist outside of that! So, I cannot reasonably expect the temporalist to accept the 'non-oddity' of my locution by appealing to this, which he or she will take as not being a case where one should be using the locution 'at times but not within time' either. And he or she will not accept that the time case is analogous to space; his or her position is precisely that God's relationship to space is *not* analogous to His relationship to time. Perhaps he or she will concede that God's/metaphysical time exists at all times but not within time. If so, then he or she cannot sincerely press a Mullins-style criticism of such talk as being empty. See also G. Oppy, *Describing Gods* (Cambridge: Cambridge University Press, 2014), 191–2.

transcend perfectly created time. As long as we can justify failing to categorise time as a thing, then we need have no fear on this front that we cannot continue to think of God as fully transcendent. And it is not clear that time is even a concrete thing; it's even more dubiously a substantial thing. The temporalist then says that God exists everlastingly – in both the forwards and backwards directions. God can thus non-problematically be said to exist at all times.

These two views then are both, I suggest, logically consistent; neither entails a contradiction. I hope my attempts at explicating how these two views are best understood have been helpful, but if my attempts at explicating either or both have introduced contradictions, the fault is mine. Presuming He exists, either view could be true of God as a matter of logic, but of course it cannot be that both views are true of God as a matter of fact. We must choose (or remain agnostic). Can we reasonably prefer either the atemporalist conception or the temporalist one? To this question, we now turn.

2 An Omniscient, Omnipotent, Perfectly Good Person

Caricatures

Caricatures can be helpful. Of the atemporalist model, Swinburne at one stage says the following.

> If God had ... fixed his intentions 'from all eternity' he would be a very lifeless thing; not a person who reacts to men with sympathy or anger, pardoning and chastening because he chooses to there and then ... if God did not change at all, he could not think now of this, now of that. His thoughts would be one thought which lasted for ever.[33]

One can niggle away at some of this. I shall do so.

It is true to say that, on the atemporalist model, God does have a fixed mental life in eternity – 'from all eternity', if one wishes – but to derive from this that the atemporalist should describe Him as lifeless requires a definition of life. Life is most naturally taken as a biological category and thus, on both atemporalist and temporalist accounts, God is, strictly speaking, lifeless. Whether or not the atemporalist should accept that God is 'lifeless' in the more casual (and pejorative) sense which we may suppose Swinburne has in mind is of course a point at issue; it is a point to which we shall return. It certainly cannot be said that the atemporalist must say that God does not react to men (and indeed women; and indeed those persons who may not be identified as either men or women) with sympathy and anger. The atemporalist may say that God eternally

---

[33] Swinburne, *Coherence of Theism*, 221. This is a quotation from the first edition, but he makes similar claims in the second.

feels sympathy for anyone (and anything?) for whom (or which) it is right for Him to feel sympathy and He eternally feels anger towards anyone (and anything?) towards whom or which it is right for Him to feel anger.[34] And it is not that, on the atemporalist model, God cannot eternally pardon, chasten and so on, even if it is true that God does not choose to do whatever it is He does choose to do in these respects 'there and then', in the sense of at particular places and times. Rather, it is the effects of His eternally choosing to do whatever He does eternally choose to do in these respects that is what may be felt at particular 'theres and thens'. God may, for example, eternally decree to chasten Swinburne in 2007 and pardon Swinburne in 2017 and Swinburne thus change in time as a result of this timeless willing. As Helm puts it, God 'may have timeless purposes, purposes which are brought about in time, that is, in the temporal order of his creation. These effects, it may be supposed, come about as a result of the eternal being's purposes, but they do not come about after those eternal purposes, nor are they contemporaneous with them.'[35] Returning to Swinburne, it is also true that, on the atemporalist model, God does not change at all, that He cannot think of one thing now and another thing later. But it does not follow from this, as Swinburne asserts, that God can only have one thought (we, after all, can hold several thoughts in mind at once; we don't have to have thoughts sequentially) and of course it's not true that His 'one thought' (if that is indeed how we wish to refer to His unitary consciousness) 'lasts forever'; talk of things in God 'lasting' and being 'forever' is temporalist talk. So, as I say, one can niggle away at the details of Swinburne's claims here. But one must also concede, I think, that, even if something of a caricature, there is truth in Swinburne's picture.

It seems to me that arguments which seek to show that there could not be an atemporal person fail, but that, as they do so, they reveal great differences between what it is like to be an atemporal person and what it is like to be temporal people such as ourselves. Considerations of space mean that I cannot get into such arguments now, but the general approach that I would endorse for refuting them may easily be guessed at by looking back at what I described as the essential attributes of personhood in the previous chapter and realising that none of them require temporality for their instantiation. I do not say that this realisation is in all cases instant; reflection is needed to see that a person need not occupy a temporal point of view.[36]

---

[34] It seems to me, *pace* Swinburne, that there is in fact probably nothing about which it is right for God to feel anger.

[35] P. Helm, *Eternal God* (Oxford: Oxford University Press, 2010), 63.

[36] Leftow, for one, does an excellent job in aiding this reflection with chapter 13 of his *Time and Eternity* (B. Leftow, *Time and Eternity* (New York: Cornell University Press, 1991), 283–312).

We humans remember some things; we forget others; we anticipate some things; others surprise us; we formulate our intentions; then act; and then we (sometimes) observe the consequences of our actions and find of some of our actions that they fulfil the descriptions under which we willed them and of others that they do not. The atemporal God is not like us in any of these ways. He never remembers anything. rather, everything He knows (and that is everything that can be known) is eternally before His consciousness. *A fortiori*, then, He never forgets anything. He does not anticipate anything in the sense of having a prior belief about some future happening; He atemporally knows of all happenings that they happen when they do. Nothing then either conforms to His prior expectations (He has none) and nothing, by failing to conform, surprises Him; everything has been, is and will be exactly as He eternally thinks it to have been, to be and will be. And although it is true that the atemporal God knows what is happening at every space and time and can act at every space and time (indeed it is true on my own minority view that this means He is *literally* at every space and time), He is not within space and time as we are, limited to a particular space and to a particular time, the here and the now. We are somewhere and, by being wherever we are, we fail to be somewhere else; we do not yet grasp tomorrow, but yesterday we have already lost. God has nothing of that in Him. And when in space and time the effect of some eternal willing of His takes place, it does so inescapably under the description that He from eternity willed it under, for there are none of its properties that He does not know of in willing it; all its antecedents and all its consequences are equally before His knowing mind. 'All at once, in eternity, God knows all that He ever knows, including events that are to us future, and God wills all that He ever wills, including His responses to prayers we have not yet prayed and decisions we have not yet made. All at once, in eternity, our acts meet His responses, and His responses elicit our further acts, and our lives are played out.'[37] We are not like this. And thus the temporalist's God is a lot more like us in these respects than is the atemporalist's God. To all of us this makes the temporal God easier to imagine. To some temperaments, this makes the temporal God seem greater. To others, less great. We'll be discussing into which camp we have most reasons to place ourselves as this chapter goes on, but, for now, we can, I think, bring out the difference between the atemporal God and the temporal God that is most cogent to the temperamental reaction that leads some people to prefer the temporal God by thinking about God's 'responses' (if indeed we may count them as that) to our petitionary prayers and to our actions more generally. Let's start from the

---

[37] Leftow, *Time and Eternity*, 360.

common ground given by the concept of God on which all theists agree and move on from there.

Atemporalist and temporalist alike accept that God is immutable in His perfect moral character. And they may both add to this the thought that what it is that a being with perfect moral character will do may depend in part on what we ask for in prayer and by how it is that we in general behave. If we have behaved badly, for example, at time t, a bit of chastening of us at time $t + 1$ might well be most appropriate; if we've then prayed for forgiveness at $t + 2$, a bit of divine pardoning might be in order shortly thereafter; and so forth. So, atemporalist and temporalist alike can agree that (a) God's general intention to do what perfect goodness requires is immutable; and (b) the particular intentions this general intention gives rise to depend in part on us. But the nature of this dependence will be understood differently by the atemporalist and temporalist; for the atemporalist, God's particular intentions too are immutable; not so for the temporalist; for the atemporalist our prayers don't change God; for the temporalist, they do.[38]

On atemporalism, God eternally intends, say, to chasten me on date y and pardon me on date z, but His eternally intending this has the following counterfactual aspect: if I hadn't sinned on date x, then God would not have chastened me on date y; if I hadn't repented on date y (I was pretty quick about it; that's what chastening does for me), then He wouldn't have pardoned me on date z. But, it's me who is changing during all this, not God. According to all, God's essential property of perfect goodness is immutable, but, according to the atemporalist, so too are these accidental properties of His, the ones that He has because of His essential property of perfect goodness and His relations to the created order in general and, in this particular example, to me. These properties are accidental because they could have been otherwise. If, say, God had created another universe in which all His creatures were impeccable, then they would have been otherwise. Even given the general parameters set by the existence of this universe, it's true that if I hadn't sinned at x and so on, which was – *ex hypothesi* – possible, then He wouldn't in fact have had the properties that He does have, of chastening me at y and pardoning me at z. But, according to the atemporalist, it is just the temporal manifestations of His atemporal will to chasten me at y and pardon me at z that are respectively at y and at z. Petitionary prayer and our actions can change us; they can be a part of the story told using counterfactuals of why God changes us in the ways that He does; but they do not in any respect change God. It is like this.

---

[38] Or at least it is a metaphysical possibility that they can. The temporalist need not in consistency say that our prayers do change God, but I take it as a dialectical advantage in this context for him or her to assert that they do, to play on the truth in Swinburne's caricature.

Imagine visiting a gallery to look at a particular sculpture. The precise nature of this sculpture isn't essential for the purposes of this thought experiment, but, in order to make the example vivid, suppose it is a modern piece made up of a dozen or so life-size figures, in various groupings and poses, clustering in the middle of an otherwise bare room in the gallery. The figures are carved in the classical tradition, naturalistically from stone, and the piece is entitled 'Jesus Teaching His Disciples'. One walks slowly around and through this complex statue. Following some advice given in some accompanying notes, one attends to different figures as one does so and one asks different questions of them and of the composition as a whole. For example, the figure which one – only after some time and tentatively – identifies as that of Jesus seems to be harder to get to than the others, being crowded in on somewhat by the others. Is this deliberate? If so, what is it trying to say? And why is it not less ambiguous that this figure is Jesus, anyway? The way in which the statue affects one thus changes as one interacts with it, the nature of the change being determined in part by the unchanging nature of the statue and in part by one's own changing angles on it, angles in both the literal and figurative senses. One leaves the gallery changed by the artwork. Perhaps one even leaves improved by it. But the statue itself has not been changed at all by any of this. It remains exactly as it always was. And, to return to Swinburne, even the most lifelike statue can seem a bit, well, lifeless.

Omniscience

God is traditionally said to know everything. Of course, one needs to clarify immediately – quite what should one have in mind with 'everything'? Over what is one quantifying? First, it is a commonplace to observe in this connection that God cannot be said to have 'know-how' knowledge – for example, to know how to juggle six balls at once. Knowing how to do a particular activity is having the relevant skill and God possesses no skills. (It should be noted that this is no real limitation; He does not need to possess skills as He is able to bring about directly any effect He may wish to bring about. And God does know everything that there is to know about skills – the physics of juggling; and so on.) Second, God cannot be said to have knowledge *by acquaintance* of some feelings – the sort of feelings a perfect person could never have – for example, the sort of thing that I might express were I to say the following, 'Believe me, I know exactly what it feels like suddenly to realise that one's made an egregious philosophical blunder among far greater minds than one's own.' But, then again, God will know everything about such feelings, everything that is which can be known by anyone who has never themselves had such feelings.

And that may well be all that there is to know about them. 'Believe me', He may say to me one day, 'I too know just what it feels like to have made an egregious philosophical blunder among far greater minds than one's own, just not – as in your case – as a result of having experienced it or anything like it myself.' That may be all that there is to know about such feelings, but it may not. If it is not, that is plausibly because there is some residual 'qualia-tative' element to feelings of at least some sorts, an element that one can only (as a matter of logical or metaphysical necessity) come to know about by oneself feeling it. And, if this is so, then this thing cannot, *ex hypothesi*, be encapsulated in a proposition (as, if it were to be capable of such encapsulation, it could be conveyed to a mind that had never had the feeling), and thus God cannot be said to know about the 'qualia-tative' element of any feelings which it is impossible for a perfect person to have, e.g. acute embarrassment.[39] Even then, God would still know all expressible truths about all feelings.

These two points (and similar considerations) push the consensus, quite rightly it seems to me, towards thinking of God's knowledge as propositional or at least as being able to be cashed out (at least in part)[40] in propositional terms. God knows everything is (or entails) its being true that for all true propositions, God knows that they are true. There is controversy about (a) whether or not propositions exist and (b) how they are to be understood, even if it is granted that they exist; and the concerns behind such questions obviously interrelate. There are also some set-theoretic worries; perhaps there cannot be a set of all truths, in which case it's not even logically possible for a being to know the set of all truths, though arguments to this conclusion may be doubted. In any case, considerations of space mean that I shall pass such controversies by and continue to suppose that this, which one may with justification call 'the standard' account of omniscience, may be defended against such concerns. I wish to focus instead on what I shall contend is a more serious problem arising from the divine attribute of omniscience for the temporalist conception of God. As a precursor to that, allow me to articulate how one gets from the attribute of omniscience, so understood, to the attribute of infallibility as I shall understand it.

Given that a perfect being will not be able to hold contradictory beliefs, it quickly follows from God's knowing of all true propositions that they are true that He believes no falsehoods and that God knows of Himself that He knows all truths and believes no falsehoods. God also knows of Himself that He has the property of believing all truths and no falsehoods essentially, as it is true

---

[39] The Doctrine of the Trinity may provide some options here, ones that I shall not explore.

[40] See C. Taliaferro, 'Divine Cognitive Power', *International Journal for Philosophy of Religion* (1985), 14, 133–40, for something one might wish to add.

that He does have this property essentially; and He also knows that He is a necessary being, as it is true that He is. Thus, He knows that there's no possibility of its ever not being such that He believes all truths and no falsehoods. He thus knows of Himself that He is what we might call 'infallible'. God's being infallible is perhaps most naturally taken – given its etymology – as it's not even being possible for Him to be in error about anything, but, in the sense intended here, the divine attribute of infallibility is somewhat wider than that; it's God's not being able to fail to believe the truth about everything (which entails infallibility in the narrower sense, viz. incapacity to believe a falsehood about anything).[41] The atemporalist can assert that God is omniscient in the standard sense and thus infallible in this sense and then move on. The temporalist must delay to qualify these claims. Here's why.

Each of us can make some true claims about what will happen at times that are, to us, future. So, for example, I am typing this in Oxford in the morning of 29 September 2017. This afternoon, I shall travel to London to have a discussion of topics on natural theology with some other philosophers and then dinner with them thereafter in the Athenaeum. So, I would say, I know now that by the end of the day I'll have had an interesting discussion and a good dinner. One can wonder whether or not I really know these things about my future now, before I've even set out – perhaps no trains will be running; perhaps I've got the date wrong and it's next week that we've arranged to meet; perhaps my fellow philosophers will have developed a passion for tiddlywinks and only be able to talk about that as I vainly try to steer them to philosophical topics; perhaps the kitchens at the Athenaeum will be closed due to a fire and we'll all end up queuing outside the nearest kebab van. And one can perplex oneself at a higher level with the problem of induction. But we do in ordinary life take ourselves to know of some propositions about the future that they are true, know them only fallibly to be sure (there remains the possibility of error), but know them nonetheless. Though it's controversial,[42] let's suppose that we are right so to take ourselves; and, simply to illustrate the point at issue, let's suppose that I know these particular things about my future now, in the morning of the day in question. Given this, it prima facie appears that we should say that God's omniscience must entail that He knows that I will have an interesting discussion and a good dinner in London this evening, and, in God's case, unlike my own, that He knows these things infallibly. On atemporalism, there's no reason to retreat from this position. For me, as I type, this is all in the future. For me

---

[41] In fact, the narrower sense is only dubiously more natural (however etymologically justified). If we define infallibility merely as the inability to have false beliefs, then my toaster is infallible.

[42] Some indeed would deny that there even are true propositions about the future, let alone ones that are currently knowably true. They would say that the future is alethically open.

revisiting this paragraph in a few days' time (as I anticipate I shall) to revise it, all of it will be in the past. For the atemporal God, it is neither in the future, present or past; He eternally knows all that there is to know – that Tim Mawson has an interesting discussion of natural theological topics and then dinner in London on the afternoon/evening of the 29 September 2017.[43] He knows it and He knows without possibility of error; He is infallible.

The temporalist has an immediate problem here, presuming that he or she wishes to maintain a libertarian account of the nature of freedom; see God and us as free; and hold that there are some knowably true propositions about the future. Again, considerations of space mean that I cannot explore all avenues,[44] so I shall assume that the temporalist is in fact best advised to maintain all these things and thus confine himself or herself to solving the resultant problem within the parameters thereby imposed.[45] The problem itself is well known. If a temporal God were now to know infallibly these things about my future, there'd be nothing I could do later to make these current beliefs of His false. But if I'm going to be genuinely free in the future – free when, say, I get to the station, to choose between either going through with my afternoon and evening as planned or instead turning on my heel and going home to the domestic bliss that is the alternative (hearing from my children about whatever television programmes interest them most and microwaving something for myself to eat) – then I have to have it genuinely in my power at the relevant time to do other than whatever it is I end up doing. In the case of this example, I have to have it in my power, when I get to the station, either to go on or to turn and go home. Therefore, if God is temporal and infallibly omniscient about the future, nobody can be free. It is worth pointing out that this applies even *sans* creation. An infallibly omniscient temporal God could not Himself be free, already knowing without possibility of error, as He would, everything about what it is He would 'choose' in the future.[46]

---

[43] If one has reason to prefer presentism, it could be questioned that this is all that there is to know; God also needs to know that this is now the future.

[44] One avenue that I can only glance down but that is worth signposting as it currently receives a lot of attention in the literature is Molinism; sadly, to my eyes, it seems clearly a dead end.

[45] To underscore one point then: I am not considering the options that would available were one to see the future as alethically open.

[46] One might maintain that the same issues affect the atemporalist. On the atemporalist account, doesn't God eternally know the truth of the proposition that Tim enjoys discussion and dinner in London on the evening of 29 Sept. 2017? Doesn't He eternally know whatever it is He ever chooses to do? Yes, but there is a crucial 'order of explanation' option for the atemporalist that is not open for the temporalist, the latter of whom – if he or she were to ascribe infallible knowledge of what will happen to God – must place the relevant beliefs prior to the time at which the events they concern occur. According to the atemporalist, there is able to be dependence of the content of God's beliefs on what actually happens, without any backwards causation. So, for example, I type this footnote after the 29 Sept. 2017, when I did indeed go to

The temporalist has a line of response here, but it is not without what will seem to many, myself included, prohibitive costs. I shall sketch it and draw attention to the costs.

Within the parameters I am suggesting we work, the only viable move for the temporalist is to 'dilute' the notion of omniscience relative to the atemporalist's understanding of it. There are a number of ways of doing this and again considerations of space mean that I shall only explore the one that seems to me the best: define God's omniscience as requiring of Him only that He infallibly knows that which it is possible that He – temporal as He is – infallibly know. This can fairly be represented as paralleling a move that everyone wishes to make with regard to omnipotence, nobody wishing to say that God can do the logically and metaphysically impossible. Similarly, an omniscient temporal being just has to know infallibly that which it is possible for an omniscient temporal being to know infallibly, and it's not possible for a temporal being to know infallibly the future actions of free agents. Thus, God's not knowing infallibly what I shall later freely choose to do with my afternoon no more 'dilutes' His omniscience than His not being able to create a married bachelor 'dilutes' His omnipotence. Future free actions are – of necessity – those that cannot be known infallibly by any temporal being, even God. Of course to this the atemporalist will reply, 'But they just *can* be known infallibly by someone, viz. an *a*temporal God, so "your" God's omniscience just is a diluted version of "my" God's.'

One thing is clear, the temporal God knows less than the atemporal one. The temporalist's God's infallible knowledge (even if not His knowledge per se – of which more in a moment) is limited to the past and present; it does not extend – as the atemporalist's God's does – to the future. And such a limitation seems something that Perfect Being Theology would suggest we should not admit into God. Given both the temporal God and the atemporal God are logical possibilities; that the standard definition of omniscience is right; that an omniscient being would thus be infallible (via the argument given); that it is logically impossible that anyone know more than an omniscient being; and that – as we have seen – an atemporal God can know more than a temporal God and be infallible; given all this, we have at least some reason to be atemporalists.[47]

London as predicted. Thus, I may put the point like this: if I hadn't gone to London, then God would not have eternally believed that I did go to London. The temporalist cannot make a similar move (explain the content of God's current belief by reference to what will actually happen), unless, that is, he or she is prepared to license backwards causation, which, I take it, carries a price tag making it unworthy of further consideration.

[47] Again, those who favour other views of the nature of time might insist that the atemporal God knows less than the temporal (due to His ignorance of tensed facts); weighing up the pros and cons of each view then would, I concede, be no easy task. It is, after all, not uncontroversial that tensed facts really exist.

It is worth pointing out that the temporalist may in consistency say that God knows *some* things about the future or about the probabilities of various possible futures; and indeed that He knows more things of this sort than us. The constraints within which the temporalist needs to work are only that God's omniscience cannot be taken to entail that He has infallible knowledge of what will in fact happen in the future. In particular, He cannot have infallible knowledge about what future free actions will be taken and, given that the future of the created order as a whole depends on God's freely choosing not to annihilate it from moment to moment, so God cannot infallibly know of anything that will in fact happen in the future that it will happen. But one can say all of that and yet still in consistency maintain that God knows of some things that will happen in the future that they will happen. One can in consistency say, for example, that God knows that I will in fact freely go to London this afternoon. But one must say that He knows such things as we do – *fallibly*. One *can* say this, but one should not. This extension of fallibility into God's essence seems to me too high a price to pay; the temporalist has already abandoned that element of infallibility which entails believing all truth, but the temporalist should not so readily abandon that element of infallibility which is incapacity to believe a falsehood. In other words, while this way of conceptualising God extends His knowledge to things that the alternative, which I am about to explore more sympathetically, does not, it does so only at the price of making this knowledge fallible knowledge. The move that I am about to endorse on behalf of the temporalist does not do this.

Rather than saying that God has fallible knowledge of the future and thus is very likely to make many mistakes about it, the temporalist should say that God suspends judgement on everything that will actually happen in the future; all He believes that is germane to the future are things about the probabilities of various futures and these beliefs about probabilities are things which nobody, even Himself, will be able to make false by future free choices (for they're really beliefs about the current probabilities of various future happenings). For example, God knows now that it is very probable that I will go to the station this afternoon – let's say it's 99 per cent probable that I'll do so. God also knows now that if I do go to the station, then I'm 99 per cent likely to go through with my plan to go to London (not turn on my heel, etc.). He thus knows now that I'm 98.01 per cent likely to go to London this afternoon. If the temporalist says this, he or she may preserve the element of infallibility that is immunity from error, but God may nevertheless be said to have 'knowledge of the future' through His knowledge of such probabilities. I use quotation marks, as one could with justification say that this is not really knowledge of the future at all – indeed, that's what vouchsafes it as infallible. It's knowledge of the present and in particular what at the present moment are the probabilities of particular futures developing. But I think we can, without misleading ourselves, think of this as present knowledge of the future. Be that as it may, even if something with a very low prior probability of happening will in fact happen, e.g. even if I will in fact turn on my heel and go back home after having got to the station this afternoon, that won't falsify a current belief that God has about the future. God doesn't now believe I'll go to London; He just believes that it's 98.01 per cent likely that I will go and my not doing so, if I do end up not doing so, won't make it have been less improbable that I not do so earlier, so it won't falsify the current belief God has about the future (or, if one insists, about the current probabilities of this future).[48] It really is very improbable right up to my doing it that I turn on my heel and go home, just as God believed it to be, indeed, we may say, infallibly knew it to be.

To see this as an option for the temporalist relies on seeing a difference between believing that something will happen and believing that that thing has a high probability of happening; thus, God can be presented as avoiding the first belief (and thus avoiding the possibility of error) while having the second belief.[49] It is interesting that one temporalist who addresses this problem eschews this distinction. In his book *Epistemic Justification*, Richard Swinburne argues that one's believing that p is simply one's believing that p is more probable than not p.[50] But that seems wrong. As I look out of the window right now, I see grey clouds; I think it's more likely than not that it will rain (here in Oxford) later this afternoon; if I had to put a number on it, I'd say it was about 60 per cent likely to rain. I believe that, but I don't believe it will rain. According to Swinburne, I do believe that it will rain this afternoon, contrary to what is suggested by my own best attempts at candid introspection. According to Swinburne then, if I'm right that it's now 60 per cent likely to rain, then God will now believe as I do, viz. (allegedly) that it will rain. Thus, if it gets to the end of the afternoon and hasn't rained, which – after all – has a 40 per cent chance of happening, God's prior belief about the weather in Oxford will have been falsified by the way things will have by then unfolded. On this model, not

---

[48] This does have the consequence that we will end up (fallibly) knowing some things that God doesn't. Plausibly, for example, I'll end up having known I'd go to London (albeit fallibly); God, in order to preserve His infallibility (in the narrow sense), will have ended up not knowing that. I concede that this 'unfortunate' consequence of preserving God's infallibility (in the narrow sense), in the manner I suggest as preferable to the alternative in the Element, is a reason why temporalists might instead wish to go with the view I associate with Swinburne in a moment.

[49] It also needs to be true that there are the relevant sort of 'objective' probabilities, e.g. that there is a state of affairs which is its being 50 per cent likely that a given radioactive atom will decay over the next n minutes, where n is its half-life in minutes and so on.

[50] R. Swinburne *Epistemic Justification* (Oxford: Oxford University Press, 2001), 35.

only does God not know anything infallibly about the future, He almost certainly has a large number of false beliefs about it too. And, while Swinburne may be content to deliver this further blow to the attribute of infallibility (additional to the blow that the temporalist *has* to deliver of denying of God that He knows all truths), as I have said, it seems to me that it is a blow that the temporalist need not and should not deliver. Rather than following Swinburne, then, the temporalist should maintain that believing that a given thing will probably happen, even probably happen with a very high degree of probability, is not the same as believing that it will happen. It is as my best attempts at candid introspection suggest: I don't really believe it will rain this afternoon. Neither does God. We both just believe it is now 60 per cent probable that it will rain, something which won't be disproved even if it stays dry.

So, the most defensible temporalist position preserves that element of infallibility as I defined it which is God's being unable to make errors, even though – as with any temporalist path within the suggested parameters – it can't preserve that element of infallibility which is His believing all truths. God's knowledge of the past and present is full and infallible in the richest sense. He knows what I was most likely to do with my next half hour at 9.00 a. m. this morning and also what I did in fact go on to do in that half hour (which may have been what I was most likely to do at its start or something else). But God's knowledge of the future is merely probabilistic; He knows of me that I'm most likely to go to London this afternoon, but not that I will in fact go to London (even if it's true that I will in fact go). He fails to form any belief at all about whether or not I go, beyond the ones that assign what are the right – if changing, as time moves on – probabilities of my going. And, by failing to believe that I will go to London right up until the moment that I do go (presuming that I do), He thus retains the weaker sort of infallibility which is immunity from error.

On the temporalist model, then, God is best seen as having some beliefs about the probabilities that His actions will meet certain descriptions, but He cannot know – with infallible certainty – of His actions that they will meet any description that they will in fact (but don't yet) meet, for whether or not they will meet such descriptions depends on future choices by Himself and sometimes others.[51] This opens then the possibility on this model for God's actions to fail to meet the descriptions under which He willed Himself to do them, for

---

[51] I'll later pull back a bit on this claim, with what I call my 'mitigating' factors – God can reduce the domains over which He has unrestricted choices in the future and He can miraculously bring about effects if things are not going to according to His permissive will – He has contingency plans.

His actions to fail to fulfil His intentions. It opens the possibility for Him to – as I have sometimes put it – bodge things. I define bodging thusly: one bodges an action if one performs it under an intended description that it does not end up meeting. So, imagine the following by way of illustration.

You are a doctor in a hospital's emergency room. You need to make a quick decision on how to treat a patient in front of you; if you do not act immediately, he will surely die within the next minute. You can administer either drug A or drug B. The efficacy of each depends on its radioactive properties, the effects of which have the following physical probabilities, which you know about. You know that drug A has a 60 per cent chance of saving him and a 40 per cent chance of killing him all the sooner; and drug B has a 40 per cent chance of saving him and a 60 per cent chance of killing him all the sooner. You therefore choose drug A, intending thereby to save your patient. In fact, you are unlucky (and the patient even more so); that which was objectively unlikely to happen under the drug A regime in fact happens. You have unintentionally killed your patient while intending to do the opposite. In this case then, you have bodged. On Swinburne's understanding, you must have actually believed that you would save the patient (not simply, as on my understanding, that you had a 60 per cent chance of saving the patient), so you will have had a belief of yours falsified as well. On the understanding I have suggested, you didn't have to believe that you'd save the patient, just that you had a 60 per cent chance of saving him. But, either way, you'll have bodged in my sense. This example shows that not all bodging need be morally culpable. But it does seem to me that the possibility of bodging is incompatible with another of the divine attributes, that of omnipotence. The temporalist's limitations on divine omniscience lead to the possibility of bodging, which leads to a limitation on omnipotence. And even if not culpable, there's a falling short of our ideal of perfect goodness generated by all this too. Or so I shall suggest.

Omnipotence

As with all the divine attributes, whole books have been written about omnipotence. As always, considerations of space mean I must miss out on many interesting points and go to what I shall suggest without argument is the conclusion to which they should lead one. Allow me then to suggest that we should understand the attribute of omnipotence as that of having the most power-granting set of abilities that it is logically possible anyone might have. In seeking to understand which abilities are in the maximally power-granting set and which aren't, one runs up against limits imposed by one's finitude, but that is not to say that one can make no progress.

First, one must appreciate that not all abilities are powers, so it is not simply a question of saying of the maximally power-granting set of abilities that it contains all abilities. Some abilities are liabilities. Others are neither powers, nor liabilities. Thus, even if we know of a given individual that he or she is able to do a given action x, or is able to bring about a given state of affairs, y, or is able to instantiate a given character trait, z, before we can judge of that individual whether or not this ability of theirs is a power, a liability, or something neutral, we need to form a value judgement of whether or not action x, state of affairs y, or character trait z, is something it might be worth doing, bringing about or instantiating – in particular whether it is or might be worth doing, bringing about or instantiating by someone who is in all other respects the most powerful person possible.

Some abilities have their values written on their labels, as it were. So, for example, if Tim has the ability to make ill-considered and arbitrary assertions when discussing every topic of philosophical significance, whereas Richard is unable to make any ill-considered or arbitrary assertions when discussing any topic of philosophical significance, we can easily conclude that Tim is less powerful than Richard as a philosopher.[52] But some abilities do not come with such useful labels attached and thus we may disagree among ourselves about their status as powers, liabilities or neutral abilities. So, take the classic example suggested by what is sometimes called 'the paradox of the stone'. Is it a power to be able to create a stone so heavy that one cannot oneself then lift it or is it a power to be able to lift any stone? One cannot have both of these abilities; having one logically entails not having the other; and thus we must say of one that it is a power and of the other that it is a liability when it comes to deciding which will be included in the most power-granting set of abilities and which will be excluded; or they could both turn out to be neutral abilities. Anyway, we need to make a value judgement. My judgement is that being able to create a stone so heavy that one cannot then lift it is a liability and thus not a member of the most power-granting set of abilities that it's logically possible anyone might have. Thus, an omnipotent being should be understood as having the power to lift any stone and therefore as not having the liability of being able to create a stone so heavy that He Himself could not then lift it. In using my intuition in this way to understand what is entailed by omnipotence, I am making a value judgement and, as observed in the Introduction, value judgements vary to some extent between people. It's possible that some reading this will think that it would be better to be able to create a stone so heavy that one

---

[52] There is need for the 'as a philosopher' clause, as it may be that Tim is more powerful than Richard as an anecdotalist or some such.

could not then lift it than it would be to be able to lift any stone. Such people will then have a different understanding from my own of what abilities are entailed by omnipotence. So be it. This fact of disagreement is not a basis for disagreeing about the meaning of omnipotence, just a basis for concern about how much agreement we are likely to be able to achieve about what abilities are entailed by omnipotence, how easy it will be to do Perfect Being Theology interior to the property of omnipotence.

As we have just seen, there are differences between what the atemporal God knows about the future and what the temporal God knows about it. The atemporal God knows what the temporal God does, that, as you read this sentence, it's – let's say – 90 per cent likely that you'll freely read on to the end of the paragraph. But the atemporal God also knows something the temporal God does not; He also knows that you will freely read to the end (assuming it is true that you will; if you will not, then He knows that). Were the temporal God to have the same belief in this regard as the atemporal (as we have seen Swinburne would maintain He has), then, even if this belief were to constitute knowledge (as it might well), it would not be the infallible knowledge that the belief is for the atemporal God. It would be possible for the belief of the temporal God that you'll freely read to the end of this paragraph to be mistaken; indeed, the temporal God has a 1 in 10 chance of being mistaken in this belief if it really is true that you have a 90 per cent chance of freely reading to the end of this paragraph. It seems to me that the ability of the atemporal God to know the future infallibly may in and of itself be described as a power; ignorance of the future is in and of itself a liability.[53] It would have been even more clearly a liability were one to have gone down Swinburne's path and ascribed to God fallible beliefs about the future (rather than, as I am suggesting the temporalist is best advised to do, picturing Him as suspending judgement on what actually happens). Swinburne's temporal God has the ability to make mistakes, which ability – I suggest – is clearly a liability of the sort that wouldn't feature in the most power-granting set of abilities. And it is true that by parting company with Swinburne at this point and picturing God as suspending judgement, the temporalist can exclude the ability to make mistakes from God's abilities; God vouchsafes His inability to make mistakes about the future by confining Himself to beliefs about the probabilities of various futures, beliefs which cannot be falsified however the future unfolds. So, it is, I concede, less clear that this sort of ignorance is a liability. But it is still plausibly – my (fallible!) value judgements tell me – a liability. And thus Perfect Being Theology again directs me towards the atemporalist conception.

---

[53] Remember, I am assuming that the future is not alethically open.

Whatever one makes of all that, as we have seen, a temporal God's ignorance in this domain (whether it involves the having of fallible beliefs or just the withholding of judgement) leads to the possibility of what I have called bodging, performing an action with the intention that a particular description be true of it and yet that description not being true of it. And if we ask if it is a power or a liability (or a neutral ability) to be able to bodge things, while again people's intuitions may differ, it seems to me obvious that being able to bodge things is a liability. It is impossible for an atemporal God to bodge things – all descriptions which are true of each of His actions are equally and infallibly known by Him as He eternally wills them; in particular, all the things that His actions will lead to (not just all the probabilities of what they might lead to) are before His mind as He chooses them. It is possible for a temporal God to bodge things – it cannot be that all the descriptions which are true of His actions are equally and infallibly known by Him as he temporally wills them; in particular, all the things that His actions will actually lead to are matters of uncertainty for Him. Again then, Perfect Being Theology would seem to give one reasons to favour the atemporalist's conception of God over the temporalist's.

It may seem that a temporal God could secure Himself against the possibility of bodging by confining Himself to willing actions under descriptions the appositeness of which is fixed by things in the past or present. So, let us return to the doctor case by way of illustration. If you as the doctor had not thought of yourself as trying to save your patient, but rather only as trying to do that which had the best chance of saving your patient, then your action of killing your patient would not have been a bodge as I have defined a bodge. It would not have failed to meet a description under which you intended it. You didn't try to save your patient and fail at what you were trying to do; you never tried to save him, you just tried to give him the drug that had most chance of saving him and you succeeded in doing that. If, as a doctor, you never try to save any patients; heal any illness; or do anything under descriptions the appositeness of which depends on things outside your capacity to know infallibly, you can ensure you have a 100 per cent success rate at fulfilling your intentions; you can secure yourself against ever bodging.

There is something odd, but not impossible, about this. Its oddness arises from a feature of practical reasoning which we can best discuss by distinguishing between what one has most objective reason to do and what one has most subjective reason to do. One has most subjective reason to do whatever it is that one (reasonably)[54] believes one has most objective reason to do. So, in the

---

[54] There are different ways of configuring things here but they don't affect the substance of the main point.

doctor case, this was giving your patient drug A, as doing so was what had the best chance of achieving the goal it was objectively most reasonable for you to desire[55] – saving him. And given what was known to you (that drug A had a 60 per cent chance of saving your patient and drug B only a 40 per cent chance), you had most subjective reason to give him drug A. Your rationality as an agent requires that your desire to do what you have most subjective reason to do be explained by your desire to bring about what you have most objective reason to bring about. That is to say, that the only way you could have been reasonable in wanting to give the patient the drug that you knew had the maximum chance of saving him is because you wanted to save him (and, ultimately, were reasonable in so wanting, as saving him was a state of affairs it would be good to bring about). Someone whose desires 'bottomed out' at desires to do whatever was most subjectively reasonable and did not go further in justifying such desires in terms of the desire to bring about what it was objectively reasonable to bring about (and subjective rationality being the best guide one can have for that) would be at a fundamental level *unreasonable* – unreasonable, but not psychologically impossible. So, there is an 'out' for the temporalist at this stage, but it is one that I suggest he or she is best advised not to take. The temporalist may say of God that He's fundamentally unreasonable or say of Him that He can bodge. There's no third way and so again a value judgement is called for. I judge it as best for the temporalist to say that God is fundamentally reasonable, and thus for him or her to concede that He can bodge. This is in part because the dangers of God's bodging can be mitigated.

It is important if obvious that the temporalist need only concede the *possibility* of bodging; there's some logically possible world in which the temporal God is always lucky; in that world, even though He could bodge, He never does. Let's call this the 'best-case scenario'. Equally of course, there's some logically possible world in which the temporal God is always unlucky; even though He might have not bodged in any case, He actually ends up bodging in every case where it's possible. Let's call this the 'worst-case scenario'. Our world then, the temporalist must say, is likely to be somewhere between these two extremes. And the temporalist may say that there are two controls on the damage that a bodging God may do, controls which may ameliorate the worries that the temporalist conception engenders in some, ameliorate these worries as these controls in effect make it metaphysically impossible for the worst-case scenario to be as bad as it's logically possible it could be.

---

[55] I say 'desire' in the Element, but there are different ways of configuring things here too – will, decision, motivating beliefs. Again, they don't affect the main point.

First, the temporalist may say that God may have limits on His bodging. Ultimately, these limits need to extend to God's freedom.[56] But let's consider by way of illustration an example where the limits are primarily on creaturely freedom. Suppose that God's fundamental desire for us is that we each – everyone of us – be saved; He becomes incarnate intending to produce this effect, His intended description being that 'as in Adam all die, even so in Christ shall all be made alive'. In other words, God's intention is that everyone, as it is sometimes put, 'turns' to Him. And suppose that He does not want to risk bodging when it comes to something as important as this. Well, He need not risk that. He cannot ensure that in the end everyone freely turns to Him. But He can ensure that in the end everyone turns to Him, either freely or not. Of course, to really secure Himself against bodging, He has to be sure of Himself that He won't change His mind in the future and thus end up bodging by reference to His earlier intended descriptions. But if His intending in this way the salvation of all created persons is something that is itself entailed by His essential goodness, then that wasn't something He was free to do otherwise than in any case.[57] The problem we are dealing with, let us remember, arises due to continuing freedom for God and His creatures to do other than is compatible with the descriptions under which God willed His actions; remove that freedom from some domains and in those domains the possibility of bodging is thereby also removed.[58] God may be pictured as having a contingency plan for every possible future and infallibly knowing of some possible futures that He would (not freely then, of course)[59] step in to prevent them getting even worse. The 'worst-case' scenario – where God bodges on every occasion it's possible for

---

[56] The setting of these limits can, I suggest, best be pictured as being done ultimately by God's own nature, which is not itself the result of any choice He has made. (Sometimes temporalists picture it as freely chosen self-limitation of His future freedom, something then which threatens the status of perfect freedom as an essential property of God. I don't myself think that this move is advisable in general, though localised instance of it cause minimal, if any, damage. God might freely promise not to do something in the future, thus curtailing His freedom to do that thing in the future.) The notion of 'limits' can be questioned; I use it without doing so in the Element, but would concede that the temporalist may say that these 'limits', in that they actually add to the greatness of God relative to how He would have been had – *per impossibile* – they not been in place, are misnamed; after all, they're precisely what makes 'the worst-case scenario' not as bad as we might have feared it to be.

[57] This is why God's own 'freedom' needs to be 'limited'. The quotes are there as, as mentioned in the previous note, these aren't limitations to freedom as it would be at its best.

[58] This is not then failing to respect the parameters within which I suggested the best temporalist position needed to be carved out. On this model, God and we still enjoy libertarian free will. It's just that we don't enjoy it over all the things that we might have thought we do and some of the things we don't have libertarian free will over are things which, by being as they are regardless of how anyone might now choose to make them, ensure that the possibilities opened up by God's being able to bodge are limited in the dangers to which they expose us.

[59] Remember, I am not considering Molinism as a viable route.

Him to bodge – isn't as bad as we might think, for the occasions on which it's possible for Him to bodge are rather fewer than we might think. God's a gambler, but He can't gamble away the farm.

The second control on how bad things can get is provided by the fact that God has, even more than we do, the ability to put things right. When we've bodged, we can sometimes do something to put it right; God would be able to do all that we can do and more; if needs be, He could perform miracles, including, if nothing else would suffice, annihilating parts (even the entirety) of creation and starting again. The most natural reading of the biblical story of the Flood would have Him doing just that. With the exception of Noah and his family, humankind fell so far short of what God had intended for them (He had bodged so badly), that He regretted having created them in the first place. Still, a solution presented itself: wipe them out and start over; only one lifeboat needed.

God intends His chestnuts never to fall into the fire, and, if they do fall (as they probably will now and again), He'll thus have bodged. But God is as good as any temporal being can be at pulling His chestnuts out of the fire. If needs be, He'll stamp the fire out; get Himself some new nuts; and start all over again.

Is this consonant with our best understanding of what a perfectly good being would be like? Let us continue to reflect.

Perfect Goodness

In reflecting on the notion of goodness, we again find ourselves joining a debate that has been going on for millennia. And you again find me pleading considerations of space for not introducing you to all of the ideas and arguments that are already in the conversation, but instead curtailing that conversation with an announcement or two.

First, if rather obviously, goodness must be taken to be an objective property of some actions, states of affairs and character traits. This is of course terribly controversial, but I must assume it. Within this objectivist assumption, there are three main schools of normative theory – the deontological, the consequentialist and virtue. It seems to me that each speaks to a part of what it is that we are concerned about when we assess the goodness of people – the deontological, that their intentions be good; the consequentialist, that what those intentions give rise to be good; and the virtue theoretic, that the character traits that they thus instantiate be good. Our ideal moral agent then may be said to be someone who not merely intends well, but does well; and, in so doing, instantiates virtuous character traits – generosity, wisdom and so forth.

Now of course all elements in this picture could be disputed, and on a variety of grounds. But, were it to be accepted, we can see that the temporalist would have to have God's perfect goodness itself become a matter of luck (and thus not an essential property of His), dependent as it would be on things outside of His knowledge and control in the future for its consequentialist and virtue-theoretic elements. If the view sketched in the last paragraph were to be right, temporalists could not say of God that He is essentially perfectly good; and it would be highly unlikely that He was accidentally so (His being so would require the best-case scenario and, as already observed, the chances are that the actual world is somewhere in the middle between the best-case scenario and the worst.)[60] This seems to me too high a price to pay and the temporalist need not pay it. Although I believe in the account I have sketched in the previous paragraph, I have conceded that all elements in it may be disputed and, given that, a better move for the temporalist would thus be to reject the 'rich' notion of perfect goodness that I have endorsed and say instead that the goodness of an agent should be understood only in a deontological way – it implies only benevolence, not beneficence or perfect virtue. Even a God whose interferences were always bodges (as in the worst-case scenario) and whose character could thus best be described as unsurpassably incompetent would, were these bodges always well intentioned (as they would be), be in Himself perfectly good. In this context, I have remarked before on the sort of character usually played by the Canadian actor Rick Moranis (well-intentioned buffoons, as in his *Honey, I Shrunk the Kids*). Rick Moranis characters tend to be perfectly well-meaning, but incompetent; their good intentions lead to some disastrous consequences (bodges – e.g. the kids are shrunk), which then, by a mixture of comedic bumbling and good fortune, are, by the end of the films in question, luckily reversed (e.g. the kids are returned to normal size, in time for the sequel, *Honey, I Blew Up the Kids*). On the pure deontological model of perfect goodness, a Rick Moranis God would be just as good as an equally well-meaning, but – in contrast to Rick Moranis characters – also supremely well-*doing* and ultra-competent God, such as that which may be pictured by the atemporalist. This 'stripped-down' (as I see it) version of what is required of God for perfect goodness can then secure for the temporalist the essential status of God's perfect goodness, though of course I do see it as 'stripped down', i.e. false. I can only invite you, the reader, to consult your judgement once again.

In this chapter, we have seen that temporalism leads to a retreat from the position occupied by the atemporalist – ascribing to God unlimited

---

[60] Even the best-case scenario might not give Him the virtues – can one be perfectly wise by luck?

omniscience and infallibility. Having surrendered ground on the omniscience front, the temporalist must fall back on the omnipotence front too. His or her God must be admitted to be capable of bodging, that is to say performing actions which He reasonably expected would meet certain descriptions and performed intending them under those descriptions but which, nevertheless, do not end up doing so. Indeed, it is fantastically unlikely that He won't bodge at least some of the time. Having fallen back on this front, the temporalist must then either say that whatever goodness (in the sense of beneficence and virtue, not just benevolence) God has is matter of luck and thus fall back to saying of God's perfect goodness that it is not an essential (and probably not even an accidental) property of His or – as I have suggested is in fact preferable – adopt a view of what makes for goodness whereby good intentions alone – however ineffective they may be – are sufficient. The temporalist picture as I have outlined it is a consistent one. Some people warm to it and think of such a God as it depicts that He would be the greatest sort of person logically possible. But I am not one of them. To me it seems that the temporalist believes in a partially ignorant God; one who is subject to the vagaries of luck for the efficacy of at least some of His actions; one who almost certainly bodges; and one who is dependent on chance for whatever goodness He might happen to have. I warm to Rick Moranis characters; they are likeable; they are, as Swinburne might put it, far from lifeless. But, when it comes to being a perfect person, it seems to me logically possible that reality could do better.[61]

3 A Unitary, Simple, Necessary Person

Unity

God's essential attributes are far from being conceptually autonomous. Indeed, at least some of the attributes that I've discussed can be seen to entail one

---

[61] One might then wonder why, despite this, I do not say of the temporal God that, were he to exist, he'd be merely a god, not God. After all, surely my view is that he'd fail to be perfect. Not quite. My view is that were the temporal God to exist, then He would be the most perfect person metaphysically possible and my (fallible) value judgement says that He wouldn't fall so far short of the (higher, but what would then be metaphysically-impossible-to-meet) standard of perfection which would (*per impossibile*) have been met by the atemporal God, as to fall outside what I have called the 'wriggle room' implicit in the 'well, I suppose I meant as perfect as possible'- methodology of Perfect Being Theology as I am taking it. After all, it is very plausible to suppose that if the temporal God were to exist, then this metaphysically-impossible-to-meet standard would also be a metaphysically-impossible-to-be-the-right-standard standard. But in this I may be erring by being overly generous to the temporal God/god. If I am thus erring and He/he does exist, then I trust the temporal God/god will return the favour – erring on the side of being overly generous to me. That's the sort of bodge I could live with, indeed may not be able to live without.

another; and other essential attributes, which I have not had time to discuss, can be seen to be entailed by the ones that I have discussed. So, for example, omnipotence – if taken as I have suggested it should be taken (as having the most power-granting set of abilities that it's logically possible anyone might have) – entails (it seems to me) that one has the power of believing every truth and thus that one does not suffer from the liability of being able to fail to believe a truth. An omnipotent being has to be omniscient as I defined it, which in turn entails infallibility as I defined it.[62] And being omnipotent and (if it needs to be added) omniscient entail being perfectly free, another essential divine attribute which I have only touched on. This is because omnipotence entails that there is nothing which constrains one in one's actions (no external power can overcome one's will or internal incapacity prevent one from acting on one's will) and thus one is perfectly free to do whatever it is one judges oneself to have best reason to do. Of course, if one's judgement were not to be trusted, that potential in itself might be of little use; sometimes, we think of people as having failed to act freely when they were misinformed about the nature of what it was they were doing.[63] But such a line of worry is moot in this context. Omniscience entails that one will infallibly know what it is that one has best reason to do. And thus perfect freedom in turn entails perfect goodness. That a given thing is what a person would ideally do in one's situation is the same as its being that which one, as a person, has most objective reason to do and thus an omnipotent, omniscient, perfectly rationally being, acting perfectly freely, must also be perfectly good.[64] And all of this in turn entails transcendence and immanence. In order to be omnipotent, God cannot depend on anything. He must be perfectly transcendent. And nor can anything be beyond His direct knowledge or capacity to control. He must be perfectly immanent. Omnipotence and omniscience entail perfect transcendence and immanence. One can go back and forth in this manner between at least some of the essential divine attributes. And thus one can be left wondering just how many discrete divine attributes there really are.

Recalling the methodology of Perfect Being Theology gives us at least the beginnings of an answer to this question. We have been supposing that God should be thought of as the most perfect being possible. Of course, He may well be other things too – the subject of this Element, say – but this is what He most

---

[62] As we've seen, temporalists will demur here, best seeing the less encompassing omniscience that they attribute to God as entailing only a weaker form of infallibility, inability to believe a falsehood.

[63] See my *Free Will* (London: Continuum, 2011).

[64] Again, we have seen reason to think the temporalist will need to say something slightly different here – perfect goodness not entailing that one always do what one has best objective reason to do, just that one always do what one has best subjective reason to do.

fundamentally is. Given this, it is no surprise that all of the attributes which go to make God be the particular thing that He most fundamentally is are not merely consistent, but also cohere; they all derive from the 'uber-attribute', if you will, of being the most perfect being possible. Even if not all of God's uniquely identifying essential attributes mutually entail one another, they are all entailed by what it is to be the most perfect being possible. Let's call this attribute, 'unity'. Consider the number 6 and some of its uniquely identifying essential attributes: 'being the next even number after 4', 'being the first perfect number', 'being the product of three and two'. Perhaps every one of 6's uniquely identifying essential attributes may be derived from every other, but, in any case, it's plausible that all of them may be derived from the uber-attribute of being the number 6. It is very plausible then that 6 too has unity; and thus it may well be that God is not unique in being unitary.

Christians may be supposed to have a particular problem in maintaining God's unity, given that they subscribe to the Doctrine of the Trinity; there is only one God, but there are three divine persons. There are attempts to derive the tri-personal nature of the Godhead via perfect-being reasoning. When one properly reflects on what the most perfect being possible would be like, one realises that they would have to be not just one person, nor even two, but three (and no more) – three people held in a certain 'substantial' union. Such attempts, were they successful, would preserve unity in the Godhead even on Trinitarian Christianity. I do not adjudicate this issue here, but ask instead to be allowed to bracket off concerns arising for some from their commitment to the Doctrine of the Trinity, and thus say that God may be seen as unitary in the sense sketched in the previous paragraph. So, God is unitary. Perhaps one might even say that God is simple. Indeed, there are senses in which I think one should say that God has the attribute of simplicity, as well as those in which I think one should say that He does not.

Simplicity

Sadly, to give a perspicuous account of what philosophers have taken divine simplicity to amount to is not at all simple.[65] Indeed Stump goes so far as to say the following. 'Among the traditionally recognised divine attributes ... the strangest and hardest to understand is simplicity'.[66] It is certainly true that the Doctrine of Divine Simplicity has been taken in various ways, some – almost all contemporary philosophers agree – so extreme as to be beyond logical

---

[65] I am reminded of the apposite title of a book on (only a proper part of) the subject: C. Hughes, *On a Complex Theory of a Simple God* (New York: Cornell University Press, 1989).

[66] E. Stump, 'Simplicity', P. Quinn and C. Taliaferro (eds.), *The Blackwell Companion to Philosophy of Religion* (Oxford: Blackwell, 1997), 250–6, 250.

coherence. We'll get to the extremes shortly, but let's start at the simpler end of the attribute(s) of simplicity.

First, then, there is the very intuitive idea that simplicity entails not having spatial (proper)[67] parts. My wristwatch is less simple than a point particle (if such a thing were to be possible). The watch is made up of cogs and so forth whereas there is nothing which similarly goes to make up a point particle, a left side of it and a right side of it, say. God, being outside space altogether, would *ipso facto* be simple in this sense; He'd have no spatial parts. Depending on whether one's considering the atemporal God or the temporal God, it is similarly quickly obvious, or it becomes arguable, that He would have no temporal parts either.

Before we get to a discussion of temporal parts, it will be recalled that I have argued that theists should think of the universe as a part (possibly the whole (if God hasn't created any other physical stuff)) of God's body. Given that the universe is spatiotemporal, resisting saying of God that He has spatiotemporal parts then requires me resisting counting persons' bodies as parts of them, or at least as in all cases parts of them; one might maintain that our bodies are parts of us, but God's body isn't a part of Him. In fact, I do not count persons' bodies as parts of them in general, so even I can endorse the suggestion that the theistic concept of God is of a being with no spatial parts. Those (the majority) who think that the conditions I suggested as sufficient for body ownership are in fact insufficient need be troubled even less in maintaining that God has no spatial parts. So, to temporal parts.

For the atemporalist, as with the issue of spatial parts, so here; it straightforwardly follows that God has no temporal parts. Things are sometimes said to be different for the temporalist. Surely if God is temporal, He has a yesterday part; a today part; a tomorrow part; and so on *ad infinitum*. But making the case for things being different for the temporalist entails foisting on the temporalist particular combinations of positions in the philosophy of time to do with presentism and eternalism and in the metaphysics of persistence to do with perdurantism and endurantism. While it is then true that the temporalist must eschew the relevant combinations if he or she is to maintain that God has no temporal parts, the issues on which this debate turns thus take us far outside the subject matter of this work. Pending results there, let us grant that, as Hoffman and Rosenkrantz say, 'whether God is inside of time or outside of it, he lacks temporal parts'.[68]

---

[67] Henceforth, when I use the word 'parts', I'll be using it in its conversational sense, to mean proper parts.

[68] J. Hoffman and G. Rosenkrantz, *The Divine Attributes* (Oxford: Blackwell, 2002), 60.

As well as objects being more or less simple than one another in virtue of having more or less spatial and (perhaps) temporal parts, we can find ourselves thinking of them as being more or less simple than one another in the properties that they have; they can be more or less simple in having more or less property 'parts' (and in how more or less simple these individual property 'parts' are). Consider two point particles, A and B, each of which exists only for an instant. If such things were possible (of course, that's a big 'If'), then each would be simple in the sense of having no spatial parts and, on any combination of views, no temporal parts. Consider now two properties, p and q, and let A have property p and B have properties p and q. *Ceteris paribus*, it would be natural to describe B as less simple than A in virtue of its having this extra property that A doesn't have. And now consider two new such instantaneous point particles, $A1$ and $A2$. Each has property p and property p is a degreed property the degrees of which we measure with some unit, u. $A1$ has 34 u of p; $A2$ has infinite u of p. Plausibly we'll say that *ceteris paribus A2* is simpler than $A1$; $A1$ has an interior boundary to its p-ness; $A2$ has no such boundary. There is much more that should be said about these sorts of issues, but allow me to suppose we've got something of a handle on them. Call this attribute 'property simplicity'. It's impossible for there to be an object with no properties at all, but would the simplest possible object have only one property and have it with no interior boundary; and thus should we not say that God would be perfectly property-simple? Some philosophers have maintained so, but I demur.

At least if one brackets off the Doctrine of the Trinity, one can, I have suggested, say of God that He has a certain sort of unity – all of His essential attributes are derivable from His uber-attribute of being the most perfect being possible and many of His uniquely identifying essential properties mutually entail one another. In this, God comes closer to perfect property-simplicity than many things, but not close enough. Were God to be perfectly property-simple, it would entail that any distinction that we might use to talk about His 'different' attributes would be artefactual; in reality, God's omnipotence would be His omniscience, which in turn would be His eternality; and so forth. But before we are tempted to say such things, we should have called a halt.

Let's continue to suppose that God has the property of unity; there is an uber-attribute, from which all of His other essential attributes (what one might then call 'unter-attributes') may be derived directly. And this uber-attribute isn't gerrymandered as a conjunction of the parts each of which is then to be derived directly from it. So, one might say that *it* is the real essence of God; and one might express that thought by saying that there is 'in that sense' no real distinction in the attributes directly derivable from it. Again, the case would be analogous to the number 6. The attribute of 'being the number 6' is – one might say – the non-gerrymandered uber-attribute from which all the other unique essential attributes that I listed (and others) can be derived. But even if all of that were right, to say that there is thus no 'real distinction' between the essential attributes seems misguided. If we consider the attribute of 'being the next even number after 4' and 'being the smallest perfect number', those are two different attributes even though they are both entailed by one another and by the attribute of 'being the number 6'. So, I do not think that divine simplicity is best understood as God's having *no* property 'parts'. He may be relatively simple in His properties. He certainly displays a marked lack of interior boundaries within His essential attributes. But God is not perfectly property-simple.[69]

The second idea that is sometimes in play when philosophers talk about the notion of divine simplicity is that simplicity entails having no intrinsic accidental attributes. But, as already mentioned, theists should say God intrinsically holds the attribute of having created this universe (it's not some pseudo/'Cambridge' property of His that He is creator of the universe), but that He has that attribute is accidental – dependent as it is on a free choice He made. It's perhaps worth underscoring that, whatever God had done, He'd have had some accidental properties – it's not that, 'prior' to creation, He only had essential properties and 'posterior' to creation He acquired a series of accidental properties. Even had God remained the sole existent, He would still have had accidental properties, one of which in this case would have been the accidental property of not being a creator.

The third and final idea that is sometimes mooted in discussions of divine simplicity is that we should say simplicity implies that there is no real distinction between essence and existence in God. This I find incomprehensible when it is unpacked in the context of discussions of divine simplicity. But if all that one is saying with it is that God is a being such that (of metaphysical, but not logical) necessity He could not but exist, I agree, but would call this the attribute of divine necessity; I wouldn't myself wish to include it under the attribute of simplicity. I'll turn to it next.

---

[69] Related to property simplicity, there's another way in which one might suggest God is simple. One might suggest that God is simple in that He has nothing other than His properties make Him be the particular thing that He most fundamentally is, viz. the most perfect person possible. That would amount to denying that God has a 'thisness' as it is usually called. But I hesitate. It seems to me that if anything has thisnesses, persons have thisnesses and I am not prepared – as Swinburne, say, is – to say of God that He is a person but – uniquely? – a person without a thisness. (Swinburne himself starts calling God a type of 'person' at this stage in his discussion and uses scare quotes around 'person'. Swinburne, *Coherence of Theism*, 2nd edn, 254ff.)

Necessity

We depend on many things: on our bodies; on our environment; and on other people. As a result of changes in these, we come into existence; we undergo change; and eventually we die. God, all theists agree, is not like that. We've seen already how God doesn't depend on anything outside of Himself for His existence and essential attributes – He is perfectly transcendent. But one could in principle be perfectly transcendent and yet still exist contingently, that is to say it still be true of one that one might not have existed. The attribute of perfect transcendence does not imply the necessity of one's existence, just that the fact that one does exist is not a fact that depends on any other. It's what is sometimes called 'brute'. That is, at least at one stage, all that Swinburne wished to claim for the modal status of God's existence. But most theists have wanted to go farther than that. Some indeed have gone all the way out to saying that God's existence is logically necessary. Anselm seems to have thought that. But most contemporary philosophers of religion reflecting on it have gone farther than Swinburne, but less far than Anselm, holding God's existence to be metaphysically necessary. And I think they are right to do so. The divine attribute of necessity is best understood as the attribute of existing of metaphysical necessity. The consensus view among contemporary analytic philosophers is that there are metaphysical necessities. And indeed the consensus view is that if God exists, then it's metaphysically necessary that He exist (and if He doesn't, then it's metaphysically necessary that He doesn't). But not all are inclined to think that we should make room for the notion of metaphysical necessities. I have a brief argument that may move some of them. It is a sort of *reductio* of the claim that there are not metaphysical necessities.

Let us assume that there are other sorts of necessities: logical necessities; physical necessities; and even perhaps (though it would be more controversial and isn't needed for this argument) moral necessities and aesthetic necessities; but there are no metaphysical necessities. It seems that we should say of the fact that there are no metaphysical necessities either that it is necessary that it obtain or that it is not necessary that it obtain; and, if it's not necessary that it obtain, that we should say that it's necessary that it's not necessary. Somewhere or other then, we'll be needing to make some assertion about the necessary status of the fact (or facts behind the fact) that there are no metaphysical necessities. What sort of necessity is this? There are a number of options here. One might maintain (and indeed I think this is the best way for my opponent to respond to this argument) that it's a logical necessity that there are no metaphysical necessities; metaphysical necessities are logically impossible. But then those who assert that a given thing – perhaps especially when that thing is believed to be actual by the majority of analytic philosophers – is logically impossible are usually considered to need to shoulder the burden of proof – in this case, to give an argument for there being some contradiction implicit in the claim that there are metaphysical necessities. I can't see how this could be done. But moving on to consider utilising other necessities leads one down the *reductio* path: it's even less plausible to say that it's a physical necessity that there be no metaphysical necessities; or a physical necessity that there could have been, even if there aren't in fact; or what have you. And it's even less plausible than that to go to moral or aesthetic necessities (should they have been admitted) to explain the dearth of metaphysical. And so one runs into the thought that if there are no metaphysical necessities, that's a metaphysical necessity; or it is a metaphysical necessity that there could have been metaphysical necessities even though there aren't actually any metaphysical necessities; or some such. And those claims *are* obvious logical contradictions. Thus, the *reductio* and thus the claim that if one does deny that there are metaphysical necessities, one does best by saying that it's logically impossible that there be any, even though, by committing oneself to this, one takes on the burden of justifying it. One's opponent can rest on the 'innocent until proven guilty' principle, as it were, and that then is what I shall do.

The attribute of divine necessity then, I suggest, is best understood as an instance of a metaphysical necessity. All agree that God's existence is necessary in at least the sense that the fact that there is a God is in no way dependent on any other fact. This is necessity enough for some, but I have defined this as the attribute of perfect transcendence. Perfect Being Theology suggests we should go farther and say that not only is God independent of any other thing for His existence and essential attributes, but it's not contingent that there exists such a being as Him. It's not a contingent brute fact that God exists; it's a necessary brute fact that He does; and that it's a necessary brute fact is itself necessary.[70] We might call this 'aseity'. God's not only not able to be otherwise than He essentially is, given that He exists; He's not able to be otherwise than He essentially is as He has to exist and the fact that He has to exist is brute and necessarily so. Or at least, all of this is true *if* He exists – it's not a logical necessity that He do so.

Conclusion

It seems to me that the atemporalist conception of God and the temporalist conception are both ways that something could (logically) satisfy the theistic

---

[70] Leslie's axiarchic view has God existing necessarily, but not brutely – His existence is explained in terms of the more fundamental necessity that is Leslie's axiarchic principle.

concept of God. It seems clear to me that the atemporal God would be greater than the temporal and is hence the conception of God that Perfect being Theology should direct one towards. But it also seems to me that it is not that the temporal God falls so far short of perfection that, were it to be the case that it was metaphysically impossible for the atemporal God to exist (as it no doubt would be, if He didn't exist), but the temporal God existed instead (and thus was the greatest metaphysically possible being and met the standard of perfection that plausibly would then be the right standard), we should say of the temporal God that He is not really God, but rather only a god. So, there are, I judge, at least two logically possible beings either of which could (logically) be God. At most one of these is metaphysically possible (because necessary) and whichever one (if either) is metaphysically necessary, its being so rules out the other being even metaphysically possible. Thus, it seems to me that there's at most one metaphysically possible being which could (metaphysically) be God.[71] Having thus answered, even if in a somewhat disjunctive and somewhat tentative way, the question of what God would be like, were He to exist, we must be at least somewhat inclined to ask the question to which all of the issues in this Element can fairly be presented as mere preliminaries. Does God exist? Is there a being with the attributes discussed in this Element? Or are all the millennia of reflection to which this Element is but a footnote simply an extended fantasy of reason?

I have conceded at various points that the assessment of the argument that I have been developing will depend on what I have called, rather loosely, temperament. The attractiveness of the atemporalist conception over the temporalist (or vice versa) and of the theistic concept of God in general certainly tells us something about ourselves; it tells us what sort of being we find most attractive. Does reflection on the concept of God and its various conceptualisations tell us *only* about ourselves, for the concept and its various conceptualisations are merely projections of our longings, in the manner Feuerbach, Freud and others would suggest? Or is it rather that we are made by God in His own image, and thus these projections – dependent though they are on the fallible and temperamental nature of us, the projectors – tell us, not simply about ourselves, but also about Him? Even if all that we have been doing in this Element is reflecting on ourselves and what sort of person we might find most desirable, such reflection could very well still be worth doing; we might find out deeper things about ourselves by looking at this projection of our ideals than if we looked into ourselves directly. After all, the best way to study one's own

---

[71] It's been pointed out to me by Richard Swinburne that one could maintain that it is metaphysically necessary that either the atemporal God or the temporal God exist, but metaphysically contingent which. If I understand it right, this is the view of Craig.

face is not to try to look at it directly, but to look in a mirror. But given that of necessity nothing could be better than the most perfect being possible, so it is rational to hope that God exists, to hope that we haven't simply been looking in a mirror, but instead through a glass, albeit darkly.[72]

---

[72] The passage to which I allude, and which I have used as the motto of this work, has a nice ambiguity. The Greek can be translated, as it has been, 'But now we see but a poor reflection, as in a mirror' (which is suggestive of the worry that we may be seeing just ourselves) or as it has also – and perhaps most famously – been translated, 'For now we see through a glass, darkly' (which is suggestive of a fallible descrying of something beyond). Will it be as the author of these words hoped, that there will come a day when we shall definitively know which (even as we are known)? 1 Corinthians 13:12.

Bibliography of Works Cited

P. Helm, *Eternal God*, Oxford: Oxford University Press, 2010.

J. Hoffman and G. Rosenkrantz, *The Divine Attributes*, Oxford: Blackwell, 2002.

C. Hughes, *On a Complex Theory of a Simple God*, New York: Cornell University Press, 1989.

B. Jowett, *The Dialogues of Plato*, Oxford: Oxford University Press, 1875.

B. Leftow, *Time and Eternity*, New York: Cornell University Press, 1991.

'Why Perfect Being Theology?', *International Journal for Philosophy of Religion* (2001), 69(2) 103–18.

God and Necessity, Oxford: Oxford University Press, 2012.

W. Mander, 'God and Personality', *Heythrop Journal* (1997), 38, 401–12.

T. J. Mawson, 'God's Body', *Heythrop Journal* (2006), 47, 171–81.

Free Will, London: Continuum, 2011.

'Doing Natural Theology Consistently', *Religious Studies* (2017), 53(3) 339–52.

R. T. Mullins, *The End of the Timeless God*, Oxford: Oxford University Press, 2016.

M. Murray and M. Rea, *Introduction to the Philosophy of Religion*, Cambridge: Cambridge University Press, 2008.

Y. Nagasawa, 'A New Defence of Anselmian Theism', *Philosophical Quarterly* (2008), 58(233) 577–96.

Maximal God, Oxford: Oxford University Press, 2017.

G. Oppy, *Describing Gods*, Cambridge: Cambridge University Press, 2014.

A. Plantinga, *Warranted Christian Belief*, Oxford: Oxford University Press, 2000.

E. Stump, 'Simplicity', in P. Quinn and C. Taliaferro (eds.), *The Blackwell Companion to Philosophy of Religion*, Oxford: Blackwell, 1997, 250–6.

R. Swinburne, *The Coherence of Theism*, Oxford: Oxford University Press, 1993 and 2016.

Epistemic Justification, Oxford: Oxford University Press, 2001.

C. Taliaferro, 'Divine Cognitive Power', *International Journal for Philosophy of Religion* (1985), 14, 133–40

To Caroline
perfectly imperfect

Cambridge Elements ≡

Philosophy of Religion

Yujin Nagasawa
University of Birmingham

Yujin Nagasawa is Professor of Philosophy and Co-Director of the John Hick Centre for Philosophy of Religion at the University of Birmingham. He is currently President of the British Society for the Philosophy of Religion. He is a member of the Editorial Board of *Religious Studies*, the *International Journal for Philosophy of Religion* and *Philosophy Compass*.

About the Series

This Cambridge Elements series provides concise and structured introductions to all the central topics in the philosophy of religion. It offers balanced, comprehensive coverage of multiple perspectives in the philosophy of religion. Contributors to the series are cutting-edge researchers who approach central issues in the philosophy of religion. Each provides a reliable resource for academic readers and develops new ideas and arguments from a unique viewpoint.

Cambridge Elements ☰

Philosophy of Religion

Elements in the series